Kids Can Make a Difference!
Environmental Science Activities

H. Steven Dashefsky
Illustrations by Debra Ellinger

TAB Books
Division of McGraw-Hill, Inc.
New York   San Francisco   Washington, D.C.   Auckland   Bogotá
Caracas   Lisbon   London   Madrid   Mexico City   Milan
Montreal   New Delhi   San Juan   Singapore
Sydney   Tokyo   Toronto

Disclaimer

Adult supervision is required when working on the activities and projects in this book. No responsibility is implied or taken for anyone who sustains injuries as a result of using the materials or ideas or performing the procedures put forth in this book. Use proper equipment (gloves, safety glasses, protective clothing, etc.) and take other safety precautions when necessary. Use chemicals, dry ice, boiling water, or any heating elements with extra care.

The activities or projects should be read and reviewed by the student and a supervising adult before beginning. The adult should determine which portions of the experiment the student can perform without supervision and which portions will require supervision.

© 1995 by **McGraw-Hill, Inc.**
Published by TAB Books, a division of McGraw-Hill, Inc.

Printed in the United States of America. All rights reserved. The publisher takes no responsibility for the use of any of the materials or methods described in this book, nor for the products thereof.

pbk 1 2 3 4 5 6 7 8 9 FGR/FGR 9 9 8 7 6 5
hc   1 2 3 4 5 6 7 8 9 FGR/FGR 9 9 8 7 6 5

Library of Congress Cataloging-in-Publication Data
Dashefsky, H. Steven
      Kids can make a difference! : environmental science activities/
   by H. Steven Dashefsky : illustrated by Debra Ellinger.
         p.   cm.
      Includes index.
      ISBN 0-07-015747-2 (pbk.).   ISBN 0-07-015746-4
      1. Environmental sciences—Juvenile literature. 2. Environmental
   sciences—Experiments—Juvenile literature.   3. Environmental
   sciences—Study and teaching (Elementary)—Activity programs.
   4. Science projects—Juvenile literature. [1. Environmental
   sciences. 2. Environmental protection.   3. Science projects.]
   I. Ellinger, Debra L., ill. II. Title.
   GE115.D37   1995
   372.3'57—dc20   95-11431
                                                             CIP
                                                              AC

Acquisitions editor: Kimberly Tabor
Editorial team: Susan W. Kagey, Editor
               Joanne Slike, Executive Editor
               Joanne Woy, Indexer
Production team: Katherine G. Brown, Director of Production
               Brenda S. Wilhide, Computer Artist
               Wanda S. Ditch, Desktop Operator
               Nancy K. Mickley, Proofreading
Design team: Jaclyn J. Boone, Designer   HT1
               Katherine Stefanski, Associate Designer   0157472

For Kim—a big part of my little piece of the world

Acknowledgments

It is rare in publishing to find a person who thinks of a writer as a business partner rather than a necessary evil. Kim Tabor, editor-in-chief at TAB/McGraw-Hill, is one of those select few—and for this, I thank her.

CONTENTS

Introduction

LET'S THINK of our planet as a spaceship flying through space. You are an astronaut living on this ship. Your survival depends on this spaceship. You would hope that the ship came with an instruction manual that told you how to get your food, water, and air. The manual should also tell you how to dispose of your wastes without polluting the entire ship.

We can think of our planet as a spaceship flying through space.

But Spaceship Earth didn't come with an instruction manual. People are just beginning to realize how using resources, such as water, soil, and air, and disposing of wastes affect Spaceship Earth. Earth didn't come with an instruction manual, so we must write one as we go on our journey.

This book will help you understand environmental issues, ask questions, and find solutions to the problems. By understanding these problems, asking the right questions, and looking for solutions, you will be writing your own instruction manual that will help you, your family, and friends survive during your journey.

Many people do not believe serious environmental problems are facing us today. Why not? Most people must actually see a change occur to believe it is really happening. The changes we

What's the problem?

People have short attention spans and usually wait until the damage has been done before they take any action to fix a problem.

are making to our planet, such as increased air, water, and soil pollution, occur too slowly for us to see it happening. People aren't interested in events that take too long to occur. Seeing these environmental changes take place is like watching a plant grow. People have too short an attention span to do so and become concerned only when the plant begins to wilt and die.

Humans are the only organisms on the planet capable of controlling their environment instead of simply living in it. People have been able to control their environment for a long time without causing any obvious harm to the planet. Recently, however, it appears that we have been causing serious problems. These problems can be placed into two major categories: the extensive use of resources, such as water and minerals, and the pollution caused by this use. Both don't necessarily have to destroy our planet if the damage is kept within limits. Nature has an amazing ability to bounce back from the changes we make and the harm we inflict.

More and more, however, the speed with which we use our natural resources and pollute the air, water, and soil is making it impossible for nature to bounce back. People clear all the trees from a forest, remove all the soil from the land, and catch all of the fish from portions of the oceans without concern for nature's ability to restore them.

A little history of environmental concern

Thirty years ago, Rachel Carson wrote a famous book titled *Silent Spring*. When this book was written, pesticides were

Clear-cutting is a logging practice that removes every single tree in a forest, making it difficult for nature to bounce back.

believed to be the perfect solution to controlling insect pests. Rachel Carson researched the use of these pesticides and proved that they were killing or making ill not only pests, but many different types of organisms, including people. The book frightened people, but more importantly, it made them start asking questions—questions about the use of these pesticides and their effect on our environment and on us.

These concerns turned many people who previously had no interest in our environment into activists—people who were concerned enough to do something about the problem. Millions

Earth Day, held in April each year, helps get people interested and active in protecting Spaceship Earth.

of people became environmentalists, and in 1970, the first Earth Day was organized. Hundreds of organizations were created by people concerned about our environment.

During the past 30 years, the wave of interest in environmental problems has come and gone many times. In 1990 another Earth Day celebrated our successes in cleaning up the environment, but within a few years the majority of people had once again lost interest in our environment. The year 1995 marked the 25th anniversary of the first Earth Day. People once again became concerned about writing the instruction manual to save our planet.

Spaceship Earth didn't come with an instruction manual, so we must write one on our journey.

Even though our interest in environmental problems comes and goes, our environment continues to be depleted and polluted. Our interest in cleaning up the environment seems to peak every few years, but we continue to pollute and damage fragile ecosystems without any loss of interest. This book will help you learn about environmental problems and solutions, but more importantly, it will help you spread the word about these problems and might even help to keep the interest alive in the future.

What is environmental science?

BEFORE DELVING into an activity or project about our environment, you should understand some basic terminology. Each chapter in this book has a section titled "Terms to Know." These sections give definitions of important words before you continue in that chapter. The glossary at the back of the book defines other terms you might come across.

This first "Terms to Know" section covers three of the most important terms used throughout this book. What do the terms *environment*, *ecology*, and *environmental science* really mean?

environment An environment is the surroundings of a certain type of organism, such as a lion, a rabbit, or an insect. An organism's environment includes everything in those surroundings, which includes three types of things. The first

Terms to know

This rabbit's environment includes living things such as the mouse, grasshopper, and grasses; nonliving things, such as the rock and the soil; and other factors, such as the temperature.

type is the living category—all other organisms that live with that organism. The second type is the nonliving category—such things as the soil, air, and water. The final category consists of all other physical factors, such as temperature, humidity, sunlight, and so on.

If you were to write down all the things found in these three categories (living, nonliving, and other factors), you would be describing an *ecosystem*. The science of studying ecosystems is called ecology.

ecology Ecology is the study of how all the things in an environment (living, nonliving, and other) interact with one another. For example, the ecology of a pond refers to the study of all three categories of things within and around that pond and how these things interact with one another. In studying the ecology of a rotting log, you would study organisms that live on and in the log, the soil beneath the log, the moisture content of the log, and how these things all interact. You can think of the term *environment* as a set of dominoes and the term *ecology* as the domino effect, or how the dominoes interact with each other when they fall.

Imagine the rabbit's environment is this set of dominoes. Each domino stands for something in the rabbit's environment (mouse, grass, rock). Ecology is the study of how one domino affects the others.

environmental science Environmental science is concerned with how people affect the planet. This science tries to identify environmental problems that people cause and the solutions to these problems. Since global changes occur slowly, the effects of harm being done today might not begin to appear for decades to come. For this reason, it is often difficult to tell whether a problem truly exists or is only believed to exist.

For example, some environmental scientists believe that global warming is occurring as you read this book, but we won't know for sure for many years. Can we wait until we know for sure before trying to solve a possible problem? In most cases, waiting for the harm to reverse itself will take as long as it took for the symptoms to appear—which means if we wait, we might be too late.

For decades people have dumped their sewage, garbage, and other waste onto the soil and into streams, rivers, lakes, and oceans. Why does it take so long for people to realize that we are destroying our environment when we do this? Why must we wait until all life dies in a lake or garbage washes up on beaches? Why do we spray billions of tons of pesticides every year when we know they kill all kinds of living things—not just pests? Getting the message to people about these dangers is not an easy job.

Scientists & our environment

Litter washing ashore is one of the many signs of our pollution problem.

This job is the responsibility of environmental scientists. They have a tough role to play. They must do three things: identify the problem, find the cause of the problem, and resolve the problem. Most environmental problems are complicated, and they require complicated solutions. For environmental scientists to do their job, many different types of science must be combined, including biology, chemistry, medicine, physics, agriculture, engineering, and earth and computer sciences.

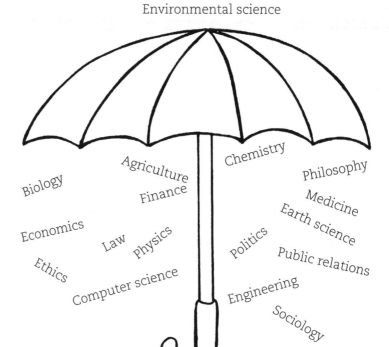

Environmental science

Environmental science is like an umbrella combining many other sciences all used for one purpose—to help protect our environment.

Biology
Agriculture
Chemistry
Finance
Philosophy
Medicine
Economics
Earth science
Law
Physics
Politics
Public relations
Ethics
Computer science
Engineering
Sociology

How scientists study our environment

Since environmental studies are often complicated, they can be difficult to describe. Three ways to describe an environmental study are to look at what is being studied, how it is studied, and what the goal of the study is. Most scientific research does not involve just one of these aspects, but all three. By understanding all the pieces, you'll have a better understanding of environmental science.

What to study?

Some studies focus on one specific type of *habitat*, for example, soil or marine ecosystems. Studies can focus on specific types of organisms, such as plants, animals, or microbes, that live within an ecosystem. They can also focus on a specific group of organisms. For example, studies might be concerned with a single population of grasshoppers, a community that consists of all the populations in an area, or an entire ecosystem, which includes all the living and nonliving things in an area.

Some studies are descriptive, which means that something new is simply being identified. The details of an ecosystem in some remote tropical rain forest must first be identified before more advanced studies can begin. Other studies are experimental, for example, finding out what happens to a population of salamanders in a drought. Finally, other studies are theoretical, which mean scientists try to make educated guesses about what will happen in the future. For example, computers are being used to try to determine if global warming will make the sea level rise in the next 500 years.

How to study?

The purpose of some research is to gain facts, without any obvious reason for doing so. Studying the feeding patterns of a bacteria, for no other reason but to know, is considered *pure research*. Pure research gives us the knowledge to move on to *applied research*, where we take the basic facts and make them work for us. For example, using a bacteria that eats oil to clean up oil spills is an example of *applied research*.

What is the goal of the study?

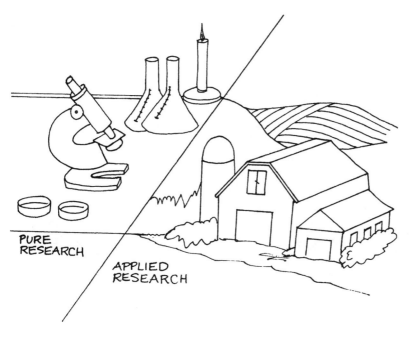

PURE RESEARCH

APPLIED RESEARCH

Pure research looks for facts, while applied research tries to use these facts to benefit people.

What you can do

THIS BOOK contains more than 160 ways that you can learn about environmental problems and do things to solve these problems. These suggestions can be divided into three general groups: Living Green, Activities, and Science Projects.

Living Green entries are suggestions about things that you can do to help protect our environment. For example, you can conserve water by placing a brick in your toilet bowl tank or check for energy loss from your refrigerator by placing a dollar bill in the door to see if it slips out.

Often the Living Green ideas can be turned into activities. For example, you can survey your classmates about the number of times the toilets in their homes are flushed each day and calculate how much water is used and can be conserved by placing a brick in the water tank. With a little imagination, you can also turn Living Green ideas into science projects.

The Activity entries are more organized and require more planning than Living Green ideas. For example, a "Storm Drain Stenciling Party" (Chapter 4) or a "Pier Pressure Party" (Chapter 6) are good ways to learn about water pollution and to do something to prevent it. Activities can also be turned into science projects by collecting and analyzing data as you do the activity. Suggestions are made throughout the book to convert the Activities into Science Projects.

Finally, this book discusses science fair projects, and one science fair project is included at the end of each chapter. (You'll find 10 projects in all.) You can use these projects as is or customize them. Suggestions are made about how to customize the projects.

Choosing a topic

Since you are looking through this book, I can assume you have an interest in our environment. Therefore, the first thing to do is find out exactly what catches your interest, if you don't already know. There are a few ways you can do this.

The first thing to do is look through this book for topics. Once you've found a topic of interest, you can either begin right away or continue to research the subject. The advantage of continuing your research is that you'll find more details about the problem. Additional research is especially useful if you are doing a science fair project or plan to submit to your teacher what you've done as an assignment or for extra credit.

Learning more about the topic

If you want more information about a topic in this book, consider looking through some environmental magazines, such as *E— The Environmental Magazine* or any others. Your textbooks might also be helpful. Also check the "Further Reading" section at the end of this book. Other sources that can help include

Many excellent magazines can help you learn about our environment.

educational television shows such as "NOVA," "Network Earth," *National Geographic* specials, "Nature," and many others. Almost all of these types of shows are found on public television or cable networks. Check your local listings to see what you can view in the near future in your area.

Once you know which Living Green, Activity, or Science Project you want to do, try to speak with someone who is expert on the subject. For example, if your project involves pesticides, arrange to meet an agricultural specialist who works for your state or county, a professor of entomology (the study of insects) at a nearby university, and a farmer who uses pesticides. If you are studying recycling, speak with people who recycle, those who don't, scientists who study the process, and a representative from a recycling or waste-management company. Always try to explore all the different angles to a topic.

Also, be sure to use any special sources that you just happen to know about. For example, if you live near an organic farm, a landfill, or anything else that can add to your activity or project, try to use it to your advantage. The most important thing to remember is to select a Living Green idea, an Activity, or a Science Project that you are not only interested in but truly enthusiastic about.

If you are doing a science project

This section is designed to help you choose, plan, and perform a science fair project for school.

Before you begin

Review the entire project with your teacher, parent, or other knowledgeable adult who is overseeing your work. Some of the projects must be done at a certain time of year. Some can be done in a day or two, while others can take a few weeks or months.

A few of the projects use supplies that are found in your school or around the home, but some require equipment or supplies that must be purchased from a local hardware store, science or nature store, or a scientific supply house. (Appendix B lists scientific supply houses.) Projects in this book tell you not only what is needed but also how or where it might be found.

An introduction to scientific research

Science fairs give you the opportunity to not only learn about a topic, but also to participate in the discovery process. Although you probably won't discover something previously unknown to humankind (although you never can tell), you will perform the same process by which discoveries are made. Advances in science move forward slowly, one step at a time, with each experiment building upon a previous one and preparing researchers to perform the next. A typical science fair project allows you to see what it is like to take one or two of these steps for yourself. The following example shows how science advances.

A problem such as controlling a certain type of insect pest without the use of harmful pesticides might be solved by a series of scientific experiments. First, field studies could search for natural predators of the pest. Lab tests followed by field tests could then be performed to determine how effective each natural enemy would be at controlling the pest. The life cycles of these natural enemies would be studied, as well as how each would fit into the local ecosystem.

Further studies might be performed to determine the population growth of these natural enemies. Are they capable of controlling the pest? What would happen to the entire ecosystem if the number of these predators dramatically increased?

Once a natural enemy is found to be a likely candidate, small-scale testing can begin. The process continues until a solution to the problem is found, and the pest is controlled without pesticides.

As you can see in the example, each experiment was necessary before the next one could be performed, and all the steps were necessary before a solution could be found. Some of the experiments might show that some of the enemies are incapable of controlling the pest. Even these studies, however, are valuable, since they provide information that keeps scientists on the correct track.

Science, no matter how simple or how complex, must follow certain steps. When one scientist makes some new discovery, others must perform similar experiments to see if the original experiment was correct. The scientific method provides steps for scientists to follow.

The scientific method can be divided into five steps. The paragraphs below describe each step. Notice that Step 3 has two parts.

1. *Identify a problem.* What question do you want to answer, or what problem would you like to solve? For example, can a certain type of insect be used to control a particular pest?

2. *Form a hypothesis.* A *hypothesis* is an educated guess about the answer to the questions mentioned in Step 1. You might hypothesize that a certain type of beneficial insect can control an insect pest.

3. *Perform an experiment.* The experiment determines whether the hypothesis is correct or not. Even if the hypothesis wasn't correct, a well-designed experiment helps determine why it wasn't correct.

   An experiment has two major parts. The first part is designing and setting up the experiment. What materials are needed? What live organisms, if any, are needed? What must be done during the project? What observations must be made and what information must be collected while the experiment is running? Once these questions have been answered, the actual experiment can begin.

   The second part is to run the experiment, make observations, and collect data. The results must be written down so you can study them later. Always carry a notebook and pencil with you when working on your project.

4. *Form conclusions.* Once you have completed the experiment and collected the data, you must study it and draw conclusions to determine if your hypothesis was correct. You might create tables, charts, or graphs to help you study the data.

   Conclusions must be based upon the original hypothesis. Was it correct? If it was incorrect, what did you learn from the experiment? What new hypothesis can you create and test? You will always learn something while performing an experiment, even if it is how *not* to perform the next experiment.

Building on past science fair projects

Just as scientists advance the work of other scientists, so too can you advance the work of other science fair projects. Don't copy someone else's work, but think of what the next step might be in that line of research. Perhaps you can put a new twist on a previous experiment. If the original experiment was performed with potted plants, can you perform a similar experiment in a garden?

If someone did an experiment that you found interesting, think about improving it. If the first experiment used potted plants, how about running a similar test in a small garden?

Brief descriptions of previous science fair projects are available from the Science Service in Washington, D.C. See the "Further Reading" section in this book for this and other sources of successful science fair projects.

The science projects in this book

Each project in this book has the following sections: Project Overview, Materials List, Procedures, and Conclusions.

Project overview

The "Project Overview" section provides background information about the topic. It helps you see the importance of the topic and why research is needed. It also describes the purpose of the project. It explains the problems that exist and poses questions that the experiment is intended to answer. These questions can be used to create your hypothesis.

Materials list

The "Materials List" section tells you everything you need to perform the experiment. Be sure you can get everything you need before beginning the project. Check with your teacher to see if the equipment is available in your school or if it can be borrowed from elsewhere. Appendix B provides a list of scientific supply houses.

The "Procedures" section gives instructions on how to perform the experiment and suggestions on how to collect data. Be sure to read through this section with your teacher before beginning the project. Illustrations are often used to clarify procedures.

Procedures

The "Conclusions" section doesn't give you conclusions. Instead, it asks you questions to help you draw your own conclusions.

Conclusions

Once you have selected a project you are interested in and enthusiastic about, use the following suggestions to get organized.

Getting started

Before proceeding, it is a good idea to develop a schedule so you know you will have a complete project in time for the science fair. Have your teacher approve your timetable.

Scheduling

Many of these science fair projects require only a few days or weeks from start to finish, but others require more time. It would be difficult to produce a prize-winning project without plenty of time. Here is a general list of things to do that you must think about.

- Choose a topic and select an adult to sponsor you.
- Buy a project notebook.
- Create a list of resources, such as libraries to go to, people to speak with, and organizations to contact.
- Begin your library research.
- Finalize your experiment and develop a hypothesis.
- Gather the needed equipment, supplies, and organisms.
- Set up and begin the experiment.
- Collect data and take plenty of notes.
- Draw your conclusions—was your hypothesis correct or incorrect?
- Write your report.
- Design the display for the fair.

- Complete and construct a dry run of your exhibit display.
- Prepare for questions about your project.

Literature search

As you can see from the list, one of the first things to do is a literature search. A *literature search* (also called *research*) means reading everything you can get your hands on about the topic. Read newspapers, magazines, books, and anything else related to your topic. Once your literature search is complete, you should know exactly what problem you intend to study. Then you can decide on your hypothesis.

Science fair guidelines

Almost all science fairs have formal guidelines or rules. Check with your sponsor to see what they are. Many science fairs require four basic things: 1) the actual notebook used throughout the project that contains observations and data notes; 2) an abstract of the project that briefly states (usually in 250 words or less) the problem, hypothesis, general procedures followed, data collected, and your conclusions; 3) a research paper; 4) the display.

The research paper

A research paper might be required at your fair, but consider doing one even if it isn't necessary. You might be able to get extra credit for the paper for one of your science classes.

The display

The exhibit display should be as informative as possible. Keep in mind that most people, including the judges, spend only a short time looking at each presentation. Try to create a display that gets as much information across with the least amount of words as quickly as possible. Make the display as attractive as possible.

Many fairs have specific size requirements for the actual display and its backboard. For more information on building an exhibit display, see the "Further Reading" section at the end of this book.

Judging

When beginning your project, keep these two things in mind: Following the scientific method is very important to the success of your project. Judges usually want to see a well-thought-out project and a knowledgeable individual who understands all aspects of his or her project.

Plastic pollution: It's everywhere!

YOU SEE IT everywhere. Plastic wrappers, disposable lighters, foam cups, and packaging material are on the ground and in the water. Plastic pollution is a big problem in our cities and parks, on beaches, and even in the country.

Plastic should be thrown into trash containers, or it should be recycled, if possible. The truth is, however, that tons of plastic items are not recycled and are not put in the trash. They end up littering the land or floating in water. This plastic might come from people who carelessly litter, from sloppy garbage handling, from overflowing city sewer systems, or from people dumping it overboard from boats. Since plastics don't decompose quickly like natural products such as paper, they remain in our environment for a long time.

Litter is a symbol of disrespect for our spaceship.

Plastic items don't remain where they fall. Plastic garbage makes its way into streams, rivers, and oceans by being washed into a storm drain, falling out of a beach garbage container, or being thrown overboard a boat.

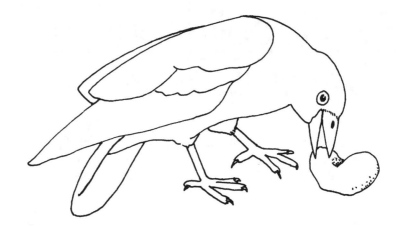

Plastic litter, such as polystyrene foam peanuts, can choke an animal that thinks it's a tasty piece of food.

Plastic items can act like booby traps for many types of organisms. For example, turtles mistake plastic sandwich bags for jellyfish, eat them, and die from blocked intestines. Birds swallow bits of plastic foam and choke. Animals often become entangled in plastic debris such as fishing lines or plastic ropes and nets, and they either drown or starve.

When buying, using, and disposing of plastics, think about the harm they can cause to wildlife. Plastic is part of our everyday lives. As useful and important as it is, if not properly disposed of, it becomes a nuisance to us and a menace to wildlife.

Terms to know

plastic Plastic products are everywhere; they make up about 25 percent of the solid waste in the United States. With few exceptions, plastic items take a very long time to break down (*decompose*), which means they remain in our environment for a very long time.

Plastic garbage fills up about 8 percent of our landfills, and the amount is growing every day. One way to reduce the amount of waste in landfills is to recycle it. Today, more than 200 million pounds of plastics are recycled each year, but this amount is less than 5 percent of the total plastic produced.

There are different types of plastic. Some can be recycled; others cannot. See the next "Bare Facts" section for more information about the different types of plastic.

plastic recycling Most plastics were never designed to break down (decompose) quickly. Plastic waste in landfills might never break down, and plastics that litter the land and water can take decades or longer to decompose. Some types of plastics can be recycled. In many parts of the country, plastics are collected for recycling into new products, and new uses are being established all the time.

Plastic products that might not be collected, such as fishing gear or six-pack can and bottle holder rings, can be made of special types of plastic that do decompose. These products are supposed to decompose in the sunlight or when they are attacked by microbes.

Plastic Pollution Research and Control Act This act, which became law in 1988, bans the dumping of plastic waste anywhere at sea. This law is given credit for saving marine wildlife all over the world.

cruise ship pollution The Center for Marine Conservation (CMC) reports that many cruise ships do not follow the worldwide ban on plastics dumping at sea. Plastic litter from cruise ships often washes ashore in many coastal states and in other countries. People who report cruise ships that violate this ban on dumping often receive large financial awards.

You can do many things to help reduce plastic pollution. Try some of the following ideas and activities on your own or with friends and classmates. Some of these activities mention organizations to write to, or you can contact some of the organizations in Appendix A for more information.

Things you can do

Avoid buying products with plastic six-pack rings (also called yokes). They are hard to see in the water and marine animals can get their heads or other parts of their bodies stuck in them. Since they cannot get themselves out, they often starve to death or are strangled. Don't litter the beach with them, since they are likely to be blown into the water. When you do use them, cut the rings before disposing of them.

Living green

The type of plastic is usually displayed with letters and numbers. Some plastics are recyclable; others are not.

Bare facts

The most common types of plastics are HDPE, PET, PVC, LDPE, PP, and PS. HDPE (high-density polyethylene) is used for milk and motor oil containers. PET (polyethylene) is used for carbonated soda bottles. PVC (polyvinyl chloride) is used for construction and plumbing materials. LDPE (low-density polyethylene) is used for films and bags. PP (polypropylene) is used for snack food packages and disposable diapers. PS (polystyrene) is the plastic foam used for coffee cups and food containers. Many miscellaneous plastics are used for a variety of purposes, including squeezable bottles. Most recyclable plastic products are marked with a number that corresponds to the type of plastic they are made of.

HDPE and PET are both commonly recycled. Scientists, environmentalists, and the plastics industry are looking for ways to recycle PS products, such as polystyrene foam peanuts, but few successful programs exist at this time.

Plastic six-pack rings are especially dangerous, because marine animals can become entangled in them and strangle to death.

Take a survey to see how many of your classmates or neighbors use plastic six-pack rings and how they usually dispose of them. Research if your state has any laws about these rings. Organize a class plastic pollution clean-up day. See how many of these rings you find. What percentage of the litter you collect is plastic? What percentage consists of these rings?

Activity

Ask your elected officials to support laws that replace the standard six-pack plastic rings with plastic rings that decompose. Some states have banned the regular plastic rings or require that only biodegradable plastic six-pack rings be sold. A federal law banning the regular plastic rings has been passed but has not yet taken effect.

Living green

Organize a letter-writing campaign to your local, state, or federal officials. Ask these officials how they feel about plastic pollution and what they are doing to prevent it. Ask them to pass laws to stop plastic pollution.

Activity

Photodegradable six-pack rings can be identified with a symbol that looks like this: < >. This diamond shape can be found embossed on the plastic. This type of plastic eventually breaks down in direct sunlight.

Many environmentalists don't believe that these photodegradable plastic rings work well. They are concerned about what happens if this plastic gets into the water, because it doesn't break down in the ocean (it is not exposed to direct sunlight). When the rings do break down into smaller pieces, they might look like small fish (food), which still creates a threat to marine life. Research is needed to look for better solutions to this problem.

Bare facts

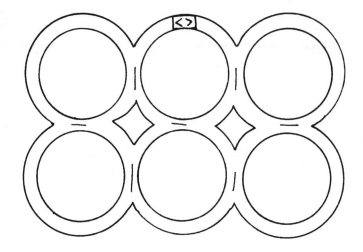

Some states require degradable six-pack rings, which break down in the sunlight, preventing the strangulation of animals as seen on page 4. This symbol is found on these degradable rings.

Living green Don't release helium-filled balloons that float away. These balloons are often used for celebrations in which they are released into the air as part of the festivities. Most people don't realize that these fun-filled floaters can kill marine life. They travel hundreds of miles from their release point and often end up in the ocean. The salt water washes off the dye, making them look clear, and many fish and marine animals mistake them for their favorite food—jellyfish.

Once this balloon settles into the ocean, it will break, lose its coloring, and look like a tasty jellyfish to marine animals. The animal that eats this balloon will probably die.

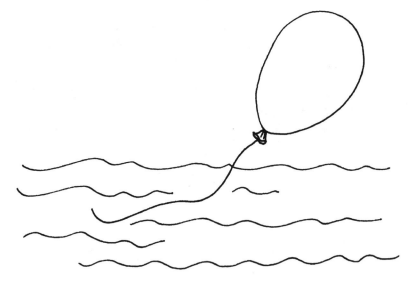

These balloons can be eaten by whales, dolphins, sea turtles, seals, fish, and waterfowl. A balloon can become stuck in the food passage or stomach, preventing the animal from eating or digesting its food. The animal then starves to death.

Activity

The next time you hear about a party that plans to release balloons, contact the organizers and explain the problems the balloons can cause. Ask them to use alternatives. If balloons will be available at a celebration, find a way to inform people not to release them, even if you live hundreds of miles from the ocean. Ask parents to tie them to their children's clothing so they can't be lost accidentally.

Try using colorful wind socks or kites as alternatives when you have a party. Be sure to dispose of them properly when done. For more information, contact Save the Whales, Inc., P.O. Box 2397, Venice, California 90291.

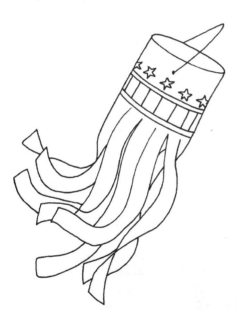

Use wind socks or colorful streamers instead of balloons at your next party.

Living green

Urge adults not to use disposable lighters or razors. Each year, 500 million plastic disposable lighters and millions of razors are sold in the United States. Many of them end up as litter. These disposable items are routinely found in parks or in the ocean,

Disposable lighters often end up littering parks and beaches.

where they can litter beaches and be mistaken for food by animals, choking or otherwise harming them.

Activity Have your classmates ask their parents if they use disposable lighters or razors. Determine how many of these items are used and disposed of each year by family members of your class. Continue by researching the cost of disposable items and comparing it with a long-lasting item. Then figure out which item is less expensive over a one-year period.

Living green Urge your elected officials to support the continuation and strengthening of the Marine Plastics Pollution Research and Control Act. This is the law that bans dumping of plastics anywhere in the world.

Living green Reduce the use of polystyrene packing peanuts and recycle those that you must use. We've all opened a box to find it overflowing with a small peanut-shaped foam packing material. This polystyrene (plastic) product is used to pack just about anything and everything for shipping. These peanuts litter the land and can make their way into bodies of water through storm drains in city streets, overflowing garbage containers along the shore, and direct dumping at sea. Foam peanuts look like food to many animals. The animals might choke or become unable to eat if they swallow these packing peanuts.

Many alternatives to these plastic pieces are available, and many recycling programs reuse or recycle those already made.

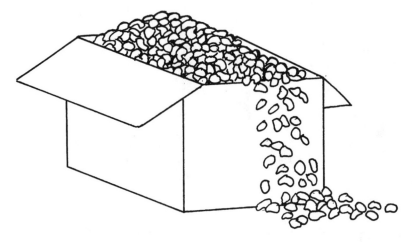

Have you ever opened a box and had small foam pieces flow out? This packaging material takes up a lot of space in landfills. People are trying to recycle these polystyrene foam peanuts or find biodegradable types of packaging material.

Some alternatives include biodegradable products that disintegrate when they become wet. For information about recycling plastic packing materials, contact the Polystyrene Packaging Council, Inc., 1025 Connecticut Avenue, NW, Washington, D.C. 20036.

Bare facts

Plastic products can be recycled into many other things. Soda bottles are made into carpet, rope, and paintbrushes; milk and detergent jugs are made into plastic lumber, flowerpots, engine oil bottles, and traffic cones; food wrap and vegetable oil bottles are made into drainage pipes and tile; bread bags and glossy grocery bags are made into garbage bags and motor oil bottles. Plastic jar lids and syrup bottles can be recycled into auto batteries and grocery basket handles; foam fast food containers can be recycled into toys, desk accessories, and packing peanuts.

For information about where you can recycle plastic waste products, contact a local company that handles solid wastes, your local recycling center, or Keep America Beautiful, Mill River Plaza, 9 West Broad Street, Stamford, Connecticut 06902.

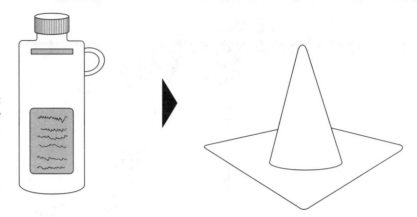

The plastic in milk cartons is recycled into items like traffic cones.

Living green   Urge your friends, teachers, parents, and companies to stop using polystyrene foam to pack everything from fast foods to electronic equipment. Suggest they replace plastics with paper products, which decompose naturally.

Living green   Farmers use many plastic chemical containers to hold pesticides and fertilizers. The National Agricultural Chemicals Association has programs to recycle these containers. Many states have already started similar programs. For more information on plastic container recycling, contact National Association for Plastic Container Recovery, 4828 Parkway Plaza Boulevard, #260, Charlotte, North Carolina 28217.

Living green   Contact your elected officials to ask them to support laws to ban the use of plastic soda cans. Soda cans are usually made from aluminum, which is easily recycled into new soda cans. Some companies want to use plastic soda cans to replace aluminum. Plastic cans would dramatically increase the amount of plastic litter that already exists and would hurt the progress made in recycling aluminum and glass. Some states have already banned plastic cans. For more information, contact Environmental Action Foundation, 1525 New Hampshire Ave., NW, Washington, D.C. 20036.

Plastic does not break down quickly like natural products do. Sometimes you don't want plastic to break down quickly. For example, the floor tiles in your school wouldn't be very useful if they fell to pieces after you walked on them a few times. However, when things made of plastic are not disposed of properly, the fact that they do not break down becomes a problem. Plastic litter, such as wrappers and soda bottles, lies on a beach or in a park for years because it does not decompose.

Consider doing a project that compares how quickly (or slowly) plastic and nonplastic items decompose. Select items that are likely to become litter, for example, foam cups and soda bottles. During this project, compare how quickly different products decompose when exposed to the sun and when buried in soil. (This project takes between a few weeks and a few months.)

Do you think nonplastic products will decompose at the same rate as plastic products, a little faster, or much faster? What is your hypothesis? Do you think you'll get the same results if the items are buried in the ground or lying on top of the ground? Late spring or summer would be the best time to run this project.

- At least six different items (preferably more) that are commonly found as litter. Half of these litter items should be plastic and the other half, nonplastic. (If you are going to run this experiment both in the soil and above the soil, you'll need at least two of each litter item—one to be placed on the soil and one in the soil.)
- An area of earth at least 5 feet square where you can place the litter items and observe them over a few weeks.
- A color marker of some sort to mark the location of each item. These markers can be ribbons or small stones sprayed with different color paints.
- Gardening gloves.
- A small gardening shovel or large metal spoon to dig small holes in the soil to bury the litter items.
- A ruler to measure the depth of the holes.
- A notebook to draw a sketch of where you placed the litter items. You'll use the notebook to write down your observations as the experiment continues.

Materials list

Procedure   Collect your litter items. You can use a plastic spoon, a piece of a foam coffee cup, and a piece of a plastic soda bottle for the plastic group. Use a paper fast food wrapper, a piece of cotton or other fiber, and a piece of a paper coffee cup for the nonplastic group. All the litter items should be about the same size.

Use sticks or rocks to mark a 5-foot-square area of earth where you will conduct the experiment. The earth should contain little or no vegetation, and the soil should not be very hard. While wearing garden gloves, use the shovel or spoon to dig a series of small holes one inch below the surface. You need one hole for each of the six litter items. Use the ruler to measure the depth of each hole. Make sure the holes are evenly separated from each other.

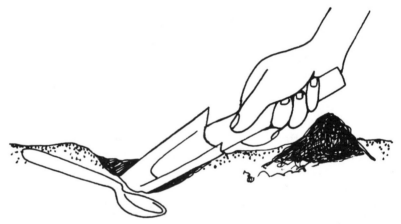

This project studies how long it takes for different types of litter to degrade.

Place one litter item into each hole and cover it with soil. Place a marker on each item. Draw a sketch in your notebook of this area and the locations of all the items using the markers as your guide.

Use the other half of this area to place the second set of litter items. Place these items on top of the soil. Separate all of the items evenly. You might have to hold some items in place or they will be blown away. Use the painted stone markers to hold each item in place. You might want to stake some items to the ground to hold them in place during bad weather.

Check your experiment each day for the next few days to be sure the items don't blow away and are not being disturbed. After two days, begin taking notes about the condition of the litter items on the surface. Every two days, observe the items and look for decomposition. Does the item begin to change color or break down in any way? Take notes and draw sketches in your project notebook. After two weeks, use your shovel or spoon to dig up the items that were buried. Make observations and take notes. Then return each item to its original position beneath the soil.

Continue making observations and taking notes about the items on the surface every two days and those beneath the surface every two weeks.

Conclusions

Compare how the plastic and nonplastic items in the soil broke down over time. Were the differences clearly visible? How about the items on top of the soil? Were the differences obvious? Compare the two groups to see how the decomposition compared between items on and in the soil. Were your original hypotheses correct? How does this information help you understand plastic pollution?

Continue this project using photodegradable plastic items. Compare these items with the regular plastic and nonplastic items.

Pesticides & fertilizers: Polluting land & sea

EACH YEAR, roughly four billion pounds of pesticides are used worldwide. Many problems are associated with pesticides. Numerous studies have found birds, mammals, and fish to be poisoned by pesticides either by direct contact or by ingesting poisoned organisms. Pesticides can build up in an animal's body and are passed along food chains to higher forms of life when the animal is eaten by a predator. The higher up in the food chain, the more pesticide an animal is likely to have in its body.

Pesticides end up everywhere: in groundwater, rivers and streams, ponds, lakes and oceans, in the air, in the soil, and on and in plants and animals, including humans. Not only do we spray pesticides on farms, gardens, and lawns, but we also use unnatural fertilizers. These synthetic fertilizers change the texture of the soil, increasing the chance of soil erosion. Most of this fertilizer never makes it into the soil and the intended plants. Instead, rainwater usually washes most of the fertilizer away. This runoff flows to streams and rivers, ponds and lakes, and finally to the sea.

The extra nutrients (nitrogen and phosphorus) contained in these fertilizers affect aquatic ecosystems by increasing the amount of algae that can grow there. This extra algae growth causes an increase in the number of bacteria. This often results in shortages of dissolved oxygen in the water and the death of certain organisms and possibly an entire aquatic ecosystem. People need to reduce their use of artificial pesticides and fertilizers to help save soil and aquatic ecosystems.

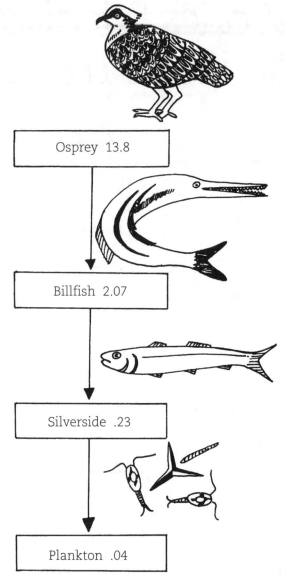

Osprey 13.8

Billfish 2.07

Silverside .23

Plankton .04

DDT(parts per million)

Animals at the higher end of the food chain usually have a greater amount of pesticides in their bodies than those at the lower end.

When people use a fertilizer on their lawns and farms, much of it runs off and ends up in streams and ponds, where it changes the natural balance of chemicals in the water.

Terms to know

pesticide Pesticide is a name for many types of poisons that kill unwanted organisms. Although pesticides are responsible for saving countless lives and protecting our food supply, they also cause many problems. Almost two million tons of pesticides are used each year—about one pound for every person on earth. Pesticides are named by the type of pest they are meant to kill. Insecticides kill insects, herbicides kill weeds, fungicides kill fungi, and rodenticides kill rodents.

In the United States, approximately 66 percent of all pesticides used are herbicides, 23 percent are insecticides, and 11 percent are fungicides. The majority of pesticides are used on only four crops: corn, cotton, wheat, and soybean. Many people think farmers are entirely to blame for the excessive amount of pesticides used each year. However, 20 percent of all pesticides used in the United States are not applied to crops, but to lawns, gardens, golf courses, and other nonfarming lands.

Federal Insecticide, Fungicide and Rodenticide Act (FIFRA)
This U.S. law was created in 1972. It gives the Environmental Protection Agency (EPA) the responsibility to test and regulate pesticides to protect the environment. Many environmentalists

consider this law to be the most poorly enforced environmental law in effect.

fertilizer   A fertilizer is a substance added to the soil to add nutrients required for plant growth. Fertilizers can be organic or synthetic. *Organic fertilizers* are natural products that include manure and peat. *Synthetic fertilizers* are manufactured. Fertilizers supply the three primary plant nutrients: potassium, phosphorus, and nitrogen, which are called *macronutrients*. They might also contain substances required by plants in smaller amounts, called *micronutrients*, including boron and zinc.

Things you can do

You can do many things to help reduce the use of pesticides and fertilizers. Try some of the following ideas and activities on your own or with friends and classmates. Some of these activities mention organizations to write to, or you can contact some of the organizations in Appendix A for more information.

Living green

Try to reduce your family's use of pesticides on your lawn and garden. Do you know what happens to most of the fertilizer and pesticides that you apply? They travel with rainwater runoff into streams, rivers, lakes and ponds, and finally the sea. Even if they go down storm drains, they will probably end up in a stream, lake, or the ocean hundreds of miles away. Pesticides kill aquatic plant and animal life.

The pesticides that do remain on plants are eaten by animals and absorbed into their body. Pesticides can make the animal sick or be passed along to other animals in the food chain.

Activity

Design an environmentally sound landscape for a new house being built in your neighborhood. Find out which plants would require the least amount of fertilizers, pesticides, and water for your location, but would still make the lawn look good. Include these plants in your design. You can learn about these types of plants by speaking with someone at a local organic garden center or your local extension service. Compare your design with the actual plants you found planted at a new construction site. (Remember to ask permission before entering a construction site. These sites can be very dangerous!) Speak to

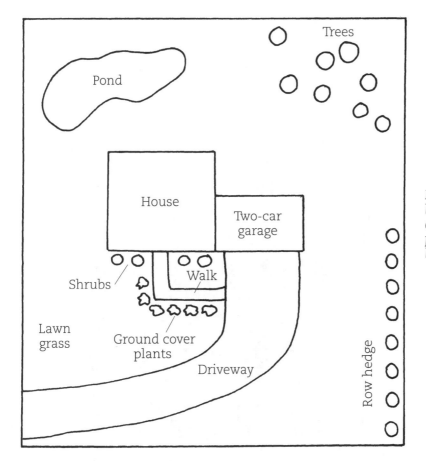

Replace the plants that a builder was going to plant around a new house with plants that require little water.

a representative from the builder to try to get the company to use more environmentally sensitive plants for its next new home.

Ask your parents to help you build a compost heap. Americans throw out more than 1,000 pounds of organic wastes per person each year. Organic waste means things like leftover foods. Much of this waste goes down a drain, possibly through a garbage disposal, and into the city sewage system, where it increases the amount of nutrients entering the wastewater. When this water makes its way into streams, rivers, and the ocean, it harms or even destroys these ecosystems.

Activity

Instead of allowing this nutrient-rich waste to kill aquatic life, use it to help your lawn and garden grow by building (or buying) a composter that converts leftover food and other wastes into rich fertilizer (compost) for your lawn or garden. This organic fertilizer is far safer for the environment than synthetic fertilizers.

If you have a lawn, building and using a composter is one of the best ways to help reduce waste and problems caused by fertilizers.

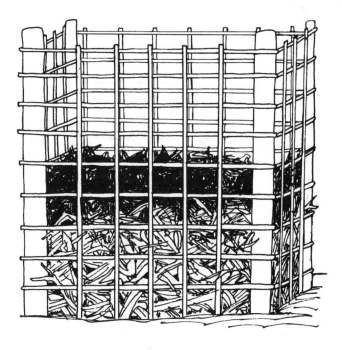

To build a small composter, follow these directions. A typical small-garden compost heap consists of a wire frame (that allows air to circulate) about 5 feet square. Place a layer of twigs on the bottom a few inches deep to let air circulate. Then add a layer of dry organic matter, such as leaves or grass clippings, over the twigs to about a depth of one to two inches. Finally, add organic wastes (leftover fruit and vegetable peelings, food scraps, bread products, egg shells, etc.). Avoid using greasy food scraps such as meat trimmings and chicken bones. Over each layer of organic waste, place a thin layer of soil (or cat litter). Continue adding layers of waste and soil until the frame is full, or at least 3 feet high.

The pile should be turned over once a month. Leave a depression on the top to collect water so that it can seep in. In 6 to 12 months the organic matter should decompose into a rich compost that can be used as fertilizer. The compost is ready when it has turned brown or black, has no unpleasant odor, and the original contents are no longer identifiable.

Bare facts

One of the most obvious forms of recycling is overlooked by millions of individuals who mow their lawns and remove the clippings, only to apply fertilizer to replace these lost nutrients. Lawn clippings have a fertilizer value of 5-1-3. This information, found on all fertilizer containers, represents the percentage of nitrogen, phosphorus, and potassium, respectively, in the fertilizer. It takes about two pounds of fertilizer per thousand square feet to replace the nutrients removed by the clippings.

Think about it. Fertilizers are expensive, but grass clippings are free. Synthetic fertilizers ruin the soil texture, but grass clippings improve it. Grass clippings must be placed in a landfill or incinerated. When used as a fertilizer, they decompose naturally.

Bagging grass clippings and then spreading synthetic fertilizer to replace the lost nutrients makes little sense.

Living green Don't waste natural fertilizer. Dead and decaying organisms are the most important supply of nutrients for future generations of plants. When left on the lawn, grass clippings decompose and become usable to the growing grass in about one week, reducing the amount of fertilizer required by about 25 percent. Grass recycling keeps clippings (which are a very bulky form of waste) out of landfills and reduces the need for synthetic fertilizers.

To recycle grass clippings, you'll need to cut the grass more often because the clippings must be one inch or shorter and the grass should be left about two inches tall. (Remember, you don't have to bag, so mowing takes less time.) The grass should not be damp. Tall, dry grass and short clippings mean the clippings fall between the remaining grass instead of smothering it.

Living green Use alternating plants (called *intercrops*) in your garden to decrease pest populations without harmful pesticides. The following plants attract beneficial insects that help control pests and reduce the need for chemicals: herbs that belong to the mint family, such as lemon balm and thyme; plants that belong to the carrot family, such as dill and parsley; and vegetables that belong to the cabbage family, such as radishes and broccoli. Queen Anne's lace (wild carrot) helps attract native parasitic wasps.

Use rows of alternating plants in your garden to help reduce insect pests.

Create an experimental garden to see the difference between a *monoculture* garden (consisting of one crop) and an intercrop. Study the differences you find in the number and types of pests in each plot of your garden. This activity can easily be turned into a science project. (See "What You Can Do" at the front of this book.)

Activity

Use organic, natural pesticides instead of synthetic pesticides. Organic pesticides cause less harm to the environment. Go to a garden supply house that sells many kinds of nontoxic pesticides. Some nontoxic pesticides are called *botanicals*, which means they come from plants. Others are simply barriers designed to keep pests out. Ask a knowledgeable salesperson how to use these products properly.

Living green

Create an experimental garden to compare the use of synthetic pesticides and natural pesticides. Compare the types of pests and the numbers of each found in each group. This activity can be turned into a science fair project. (See "What You Can Do" at the front of this book.)

Activity

Since most pesticides don't know the difference between a pest and a beneficial organism, some people feel they should be called *biocides*, which means they kill all forms of life, good and bad. Pesticides are extremely destructive to aquatic ecosystems. Some kill organisms outright while others remain in an animal's body, slowly increasing in amount until the animal becomes ill and possibly dies. This process is called *bioaccumulation*.

Predators eat other animals that already have pesticides in their bodies. This process is called *biomagnification*. Through biomagnification, animals can end up with very large amounts of these poisons in their bodies.

Bare facts

Use biocontrol measures instead of synthetic pesticides to control house and garden pests. Biocontrol uses predators, parasites, and parasitoids to control or eliminate pests. Ladybugs and praying mantises are commonly used as pest

Living green

Biocontrol uses beneficial insects to control insect pests. The ladybug and praying mantis are the best-known beneficial insects, but many others, such as parasitic wasps, are useful.

predators, but they are not the only ones. You can also buy pesticidal bacteria or fungi that attack and destroy pests and continue to do so indefinitely.

Activity   Create an experiment to see how biocontrol of pests compares with the use of synthetic pesticides. You can do this experiment in a garden or under controlled conditions with potted plants. Go to an organic garden center and ask for nontoxic or organic pesticides. Then find a synthetic pesticide that controls the same type of pest. This activity can easily be turned into a science project. (See "What You Can Do" at the front of this book for more information.)

Living green   Use organic fertilizers instead of synthetic fertilizers to enrich your lawn. You can make your own organic fertilizer with a composter, or you can buy it from an organic garden center.

Organic fertilizers come from natural products such as peat or manure.

Compare the soil on a farm that has been using synthetic fertilizers for many years with soil from an organic farm that only uses natural fertilizer. Can you see a difference in soil texture? Ask permission before walking on anyone's property. Speak with your science teacher about ways to compare soil texture besides just feeling it.

Activity

Plant *nitrogen-fixing* plants such as beans and clover in alternating rows, or alternate plants each season to replace lost nitrogen and reduce the need for synthetic fertilizers.

Living green

If your family plans to use a pest-control company, look for a company that specializes in nontoxic control of pests. Always ask what pesticides or biocontrol measures they use.

Living green

Many lawn-care and pest-control companies are now using nonpoisonous methods instead of chemical fertilizers and pesticides.

Survey the pest-control companies in your area. Ask if they offer any nontoxic forms of pest control. Find out who handles the pest control in your school and ask what kinds of pesticides they use.

Activity

If your family plans to use a lawn-care company, ask what types of fertilizers and pesticides they use. Find a company that uses organic methods and integrated pest-management techniques.

Living green

Science project: Biocontrol
Project overview

The problems caused by toxic pesticides have forced scientists to look for new ways to control insect pests instead of using deadly pesticides. Many insects eat other insects. Insects that eat insect pests are called *beneficial insects*. (All insects are useful, since they play important roles in ecosystems.) When a beneficial insect is used to control an insect pest, it is called *biocontrol*. Biocontrol can be used instead of harmful pesticides. The more we learn about the dangers of pesticides, the more popular biocontrol becomes.

One of the most common beneficial insects is the praying mantis. In this project you will study the praying mantis to determine if it can be used for biocontrol. During this project you will determine how many praying mantises come out of a single egg case. Then you will see how many fruit flies (an insect pest) one of these newly hatched mantises can eat in a week. What are your hypotheses?

Materials list

- A praying mantis egg case, which you can order from a biological supply house (see list in Appendix B) or buy at an organic gardening store. With some luck you might even be able to collect one outdoors during the warm summer months.
- Fruit flies, which can also be ordered from a biological supply house or collected by leaving a piece of fruit to rot outdoors during the warm summer months. You can catch them with a transfer aspirator when they land on the fruit. (Information on an aspirator follows.)
- 1 large (32-ounce), wide-mouthed jar.
- 3 small (16-ounce), wide-mouthed jars.
- Nylon material, such as pantyhose, to fit over the mouths of the jars.
- Rubber bands to fit around the mouths of all the jars.
- Cotton balls.
- Model plane paintbrush to carry the young praying mantises.
- Transfer aspirator to move the small fruit flies.

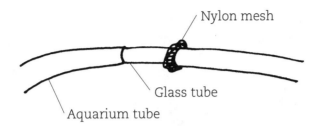

Nylon mesh

Glass tube

Aquarium tube

A transfer aspirator lets you transfer small insects from one place to another.

You will create a home for the young praying mantises that hatch out of the egg mass. You will separate out a few individuals and then feed them a certain number of fruit flies each day to determine how many each young mantis eats over a two-week period.

Put the praying mantis egg case that you bought or collected (along with the stem it came on) in the large jar and keep the

Procedures

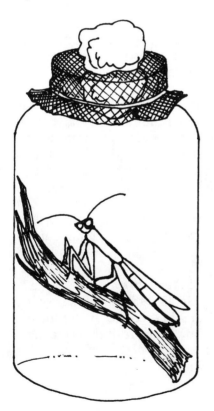

The home for the praying mantises will look something like this picture.

jar at room temperature. Cover the jar with the nylon material and secure the nylon tightly with a rubber band. (Be sure it is tight or the mantises will crawl out.) Cut a small cross in the middle of the nylon material, and then stick a wetted cotton ball halfway into the nylon. The wet cotton ball will provide the insect's water supply. You can add water by dripping it onto the outside of the cotton ball when it becomes dry. The water will seep through to the inside portion of the cotton ball.

Check the jar every day to see if the young have emerged. When they do emerge from the egg mass, they will all emerge within a few hours of each other.

Next, set up the three smaller jars like you did the larger jar, with a cotton ball in the top of each one. Place a few twigs in each jar to provide a place for the insects to crawl. (Before continuing with the next part of this project, put the large jar in the refrigerator for about 5 minutes to slow the young mantises down.) Open the nylon on the jar and use the model plane paintbrush to gently carry a single young mantis from the large jar to one of the smaller ones. (Don't worry about them flying out of the jar—they cannot fly at this young age.)

Use the transfer aspirator to place 10 fruit flies in the jar with the single praying mantis. Suck 10 fruit flies into the transfer aspirator from their container. Hold your finger over the hole of the aspirator so they don't escape. Remove the cotton ball from the nylon mesh top and place the end of the aspirator tube into the hole where the cotton was. Gently blow through the aspirator to push the fruit flies from the aspirator into the jar. Replace the cotton ball in the mesh. Repeat all of these steps for the other two small jars so you have three groups running at the same time.

Count the number of fruit flies in the jars every day. Make note of how many are left each day. Replace those that were eaten each day so you keep 10 fruit flies in each jar. Do this for at least two weeks to determine how many fruit flies a young praying mantis eats per week. Release all the insects outside at the conclusion of the experiment.

How many fruit flies did each of the young mantises eat over the two-week period? What was the average of the three? Do these predators eat enough of the insect pests to make them useful for biocontrol? Will they work as well in an actual garden? Can you create an experiment to test your hypothesis?

Conclusions

Soil erosion: Damage to land & water

SOIL ERODES when rainwater hits the earth and travels over the surface. This runoff water dislodges soil particles, which then travel with the water. The primary reason soil erosion occurs is the lack of plants to create a ground cover. Agriculture, construction, mining, and logging all remove ground cover, allowing soil erosion to occur.

Plants would hold the topsoil in place and prevent the soil erosion seen here.

Soil erosion causes two types of problems. First, the land that loses the soil can no longer support plant life. If plants cannot grow, then animals will not move into the area. The result is a dead ecosystem. People try to replace this lost soil with synthetic fertilizers that change the texture of the soil and make the soil even more likely to erode.

The second problem is what happens to all this soil that has eroded away. The water that must accept all this extra soil (now called *sediment*) is changed. Millions of tons of sediment are added to bodies of water each year. Carried with this sediment are fertilizers, pesticides, and other pollutants.

This unnatural amount of sediment in the water changes the aquatic ecosystem so plants and animals that once lived there can no longer do so. It reduces the amount of sunlight reaching plants below the water line and reduces the amount of oxygen in the water, affecting all aquatic life.

Too much sediment (soil) floating in a pond prevents sunlight from reaching plants.

Terms to know

soil erosion The movement of topsoil from one place to another by water or wind is called *soil erosion*. Erosion occurs naturally as runoff water flows into streams and rivers. Most soils, however, are protected from erosion by plants that keep the soil in place. Serious erosion occurs when human activities remove most of the plants, exposing the soil.

Deforestation for wood and land, construction for buildings and roads, off-road sport vehicles, poor farming practices, and other activities all cause soil erosion. Even though soil formation occurs naturally, human activities remove it much faster than it is created.

Areas that get little rain on a regular basis are more likely to experience soil erosion caused by wind instead of water. During the 1930s, Oklahoma and other Great Plains states suffered a severe drought. Millions of acres of topsoil blew away in enormous dust storms, and this area in this time period became known as the Dust Bowl.

soil conservation One third of the topsoil originally found on croplands in the United States is gone because of soil erosion. Soil washes away and wind blows off topsoil from our croplands seven times faster than soil is created naturally. Soil conservation refers to practices that help keep soil in place to

Although water is the main cause of soil erosion, wind can also cause soil erosion.

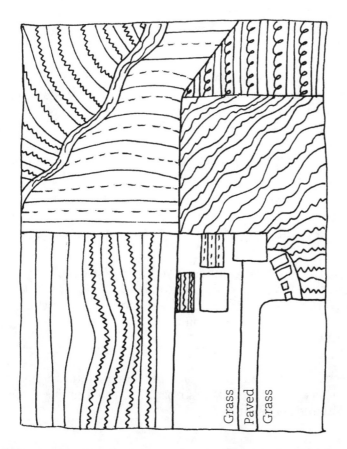

Grass Paved Grass

Farmers can use many different soil conservation methods, such as intercrops.

reduce soil erosion. These soil conservation methods include conservation tillage, contour farming, strip cropping, terracing, alley cropping, gully reclamation, and windbreaks. These soil conservation methods are used on only about half of American croplands.

Things you can do   You can do many things to help prevent soil erosion and protect bodies of water from erosion. Try some of the following ideas and activities on your own or with friends and classmates. Some of these activities mention organizations to write to, or you can contact some of the organizations in Appendix A for more information.

Living green   Prevent soil erosion by planting trees and other vegetation wherever you notice running water. These areas could be near a stream, river, or even near downspouts or where gullies form. The more vegetation that is present, the less likelihood that soil erosion will occur.

Join one of the many plant-a-tree programs, such as the Global Releaf program sponsored by American Forestry Association. Contact the Global Releaf Program, P.O. Box 2000, Washington, D.C. 20013. Arbor Day is a good time to get involved. Contact the National Arbor Day Foundation at Arbor Lodge 100, Nebraska City, Nebraska 68410.

Living green   Suggest the construction of driveways and footpaths using gravel, crushed stone, brick, or wood instead of asphalt or concrete to improve drainage and reduce soil erosion.

Activity   Survey your school grounds or your neighborhood for the amount of paved land and natural land. What is the ratio of paved to unpaved? Research how much land in the United States is paved over and what effect, if any, it has on the environment.

Living green   Suggest the use of terraces on steep slopes. You can create terraces by using timbers, railroad ties, and filter cloth to slow runoff and trap sediment.

Living green   Suggest the seeding of newly graded areas immediately after landscaping and the use of a mulch to retain the soil until the seeds take root.

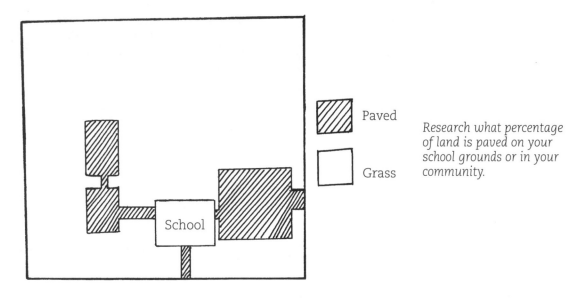

Paved

Grass

Research what percentage of land is paved on your school grounds or in your community.

School

Find a construction site and look for soil erosion. (Get permission before entering any private property. Remember that construction sites can be very dangerous!) Is anything being done by the builder to prevent soil erosion? Check with your local government to see if any laws require builders to try to prevent soil erosion.

Activity

Most construction sites require barriers to be put up to prevent soil erosion.

Living green Suggest that your parents install house gutters and downspouts that discharge onto the lawn, not onto pavement. Discharging water this way disperses the flow in the proper manner. Protect the soil at the downspout outlet by using splash blocks.

Downspouts and splash guards help reduce soil erosion around your home.

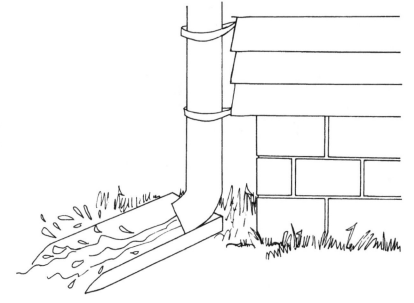

Activity Create a simple experiment to determine how successful downspouts and splash guards are at preventing soil erosion. Does the soil around the foundation of the building wash away as quickly with splash guards or do the guards help keep the topsoil in place?

Living green Suggest to your parents that they plant erosion-resistant grasses whenever possible. Try fescue grasses in areas prone to erosion, such as slopes and ditches. Check with a local garden center to see what they suggest for your location.

Living green Plant ground cover plants in shaded areas where grass won't grow. Speak with a lawn-care specialist about what kind of ground cover to use for hard-to-grow areas in your location.

Let grass grow a little longer than usual to reduce water runoff and prevent soil erosion.

Living green

Leave mulch over gardens during winter months to reduce soil erosion and enrich the soil.

Living green

Plant gardens on level areas to reduce erosion. If planting on a slope, plant along the contour of the slope to reduce erosion.

Living green

Protect riverside greenways. Join a local greenway protection group or create your own group. River *greenways* are corridors of natural vegetation that protect the river. They prevent soil erosion, provide a wildlife habitat, offer a great way to control flooding, and act as a natural filter for drinking water. For more information, contact American Rivers, 801 Pennsylvania Avenue, S.E., Suite 400, Washington, D.C. 20003.

Living green

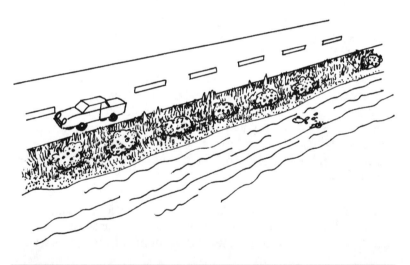

Vegetation along streams, called greenways, acts like a buffer and helps reduce soil erosion into the stream.

The top 10 types of river pollution, beginning with the worst:

1. Sediment (from soil erosion)
2. Excessive nutrients (from fertilizers)
3. Organic enrichment (from sewage)
4. Pathogens (from sewage)
5. Metals (from industrial waste)

Bare facts

6. Salinity
7. Pesticides
8. Suspended solids
9. Habitat modification
10. Flow alteration

Where does this pollution come from? Starting with the highest contributor, river pollution comes from:

1. Agriculture (farms)
2. Municipal dischargers (sewage treatment plants)
3. Habitat modification (construction)
4. Resource extraction (mining)
5. Storm water runoff (storm drains)
6. Industrial dischargers (manufacturing plants)
7. Logging
8. Construction
9. Land disposal
10. Combined sewer overflows (older systems that combine sewers and storm drains)

Living green

Support local river studies. Of the 3.5 million miles of waterways in the United States, 90 percent have been harmed by human activities. You can't solve a problem if you don't know it exists. The only way to make decisions about how a river can be used and still protected is to have good information about the condition of that river. Become active in groups that study rivers.

For more information, contact some organizations in Appendix A. Join a local organization that supports river assessments. Only 12 states have completed assessments of their rivers.

Activity

Adopt a stream or a river. Learn how to monitor, protect, and restore America's waters through hands-on techniques that anyone can do. Since only 37 percent of our rivers and 46 percent of our lakes are studied by government agencies, volunteers are needed to fill the void.

Many excellent programs can teach you how to protect our streams and rivers.

Local and state agencies run adopt-a-stream programs. Contact your local or state environmental protection department to see if one exists in your area. The largest group involved in this type of project is the Izaak Walton League. Contact the SOS (Save Our Streams) Program, The Izaak Walton League of America, 1401 Wilson Boulevard, Level B, Arlington, Virginia 22209.

Help protect remaining rivers from being dammed, diverted, and ruined by construction and pollution. Contact the National Organization for River Sports, 212 West Cheyenne Mountain Boulevard, Colorado Springs, Colorado 80906.

Living green

Dams can destroy large areas of natural habitats.

Science project: Soil erosion
Project overview

Have you ever seen a hillside with no plants or grasses growing on it after a rainfall? The hillside is covered with little miniature streams that run through small gullies. As the water washes over the soil, it picks up and carries away the rich topsoil. Without this topsoil, plants and grasses cannot grow on this hillside until the soil is replaced. It takes roughly 500 years to create 1 inch of topsoil naturally.

Plants prevent topsoil from washing away. The best protection against soil erosion is vegetation. In this project you will compare the amount of soil washed away between barren soil and grass-covered soil. How much more soil washes away from the barren soil than the soil with vegetation? Will there be no difference, a small difference, or a large difference? What is your hypothesis?

Materials list

- Two large plastic or rubber tubs to hold soil. They should be roughly two feet long by one foot wide and about eight inches deep.
- Enough potting soil to fill both of these tubs.
- Enough small or crushed stone to create a layer about an inch deep at the bottom of each tub.
- A small bag of grass seed. You can use a rapid-grow cover or even dig out a square piece of existing turf and soil to place in one of the tubs if you don't want to wait for the grass to grow.
- Two bricks to prop up the tubs.
- A large watering can with a sprinkler-type spout.
- A measuring cup to measure how much water the watering can holds.
- Two sets of large glasses. Each set must have enough glasses to hold all the water in the watering can. Number each of these glasses with a marker.
- A small hand drill and bit to drill a hole through the tub.

Procedures

Place a 1-inch layer of small stones at the bottom of each tub. Fill both tubs with soil up to a point 1½ inches below the top of the tub. Sprinkle grass seed in one tub and follow directions on the seed box for growth. (You can rush the experiment along by using existing turf or rapid-grow grass cover. If you plan to dig out a patch of existing turf, ask permission first!) After the tub has a lush cover of grass, you can continue the project.

Have an adult help you drill a ½-inch-diameter hole on one end of each tub just above the soil line. Angle the tubs by placing a brick or similar object beneath the opposite end of each tub. Fill the watering can to the brim. (Use the measuring cup to find out how much water the watering can holds.) Have someone hold glass #1 under the hole on the side of the tub while you gently pour water over the surface of the grass at the higher end of the tub.

Compare the amount of soil erosion that occurs over an area with grass and without grass.

As the water runs off over the grass, it will collect at the lower end of the tub and pour through the hole into the glass. After the first glass fills, replace it with glass #2. Continue pouring until the watering can is empty. Take notes about the clarity of water in each glass according to its number. Set these glasses aside to observe later.

Repeat this entire procedure with the tub containing no grass. You should pour the water with the same motion as in the first part of this project. Take notes about each glass and then set them aside.

Conclusions   Compare your notes. How much difference was there between the two tubs? Was the difference small or very great between the two sets of glasses immediately after the water was poured? Look at the glasses after they have had time to settle. Try to determine the total amount of sediment (soil) at the bottom of all the glasses in each set. How dramatic a difference does ground cover make in protecting topsoil from erosion?

Litter: A disgrace

LITTER IS any item that has been improperly disposed of and is ugly to look at. A plastic bag flying by on the wind, a bunch of broken bottles and smashed cans along a roadside, and a pile of leftover food at a campsite are all examples of litter. The effects of litter can range from being simply unsightly to being fatal. A plastic wrapper in the gutter is ugly; when that wrapper washes down a storm drain and ends up in a stream where it entangles a turtle, it can be deadly.

Most people don't realize that any litter that goes down a storm drain will probably end up in a local stream or river.

Litter is also a symbol of our environmental problems. A street or park strewn with litter tells us something about the lack of respect the people who walk in that street or play in that park have for the environment. Trying to prevent litter is not only a practical way to clean up the environment, but also a symbolic way of saying that we care about the environment we live in. In addition to not littering, two of the best ways to reduce litter are to reuse and recycle things when we are done with them.

Terms to know

point and non-point source pollution When pollution is produced by a single source such as a power plant smokestack or a leaking oil barge, it is called *point source pollution*. If, however, it comes from many different places, it is called *non-point source pollution*.

A storm drain that collects litter, car oil, and pesticides from lawns is an example of non-point pollution. Non-point pollution is harder to stop because it comes from many places at once.

Non-point pollution comes from many different places. A storm drain that collects oil from cars in the road, plastic and paper litter from people on the sidewalks, and pesticides from lawns is an example of non-point pollution.

watershed Watershed (also called a *drainage basin*) refers to the area of land that surrounds a lake or river. Rain falls on the watershed. As the water washes over the soil, it is called runoff. This runoff travels downhill to the river or lake. The size and shape of the watershed and the vegetation that grows on the watershed control the amount and type of water enters the river or lake.

For example, watersheds in a forest soak up much of the water, reducing the amount of runoff. If people litter the watershed, the litter ends up in the water. Watersheds are not only found in the country. Towns and cities can be inside a watershed. The street litter that flows down a storm drain is part of the watershed because it will probably end up in a local stream or river.

plastic pollution Thousands of tons of plastic products that aren't recycled or properly disposed of litter land and bodies of water. Since plastics don't readily decompose, they remain

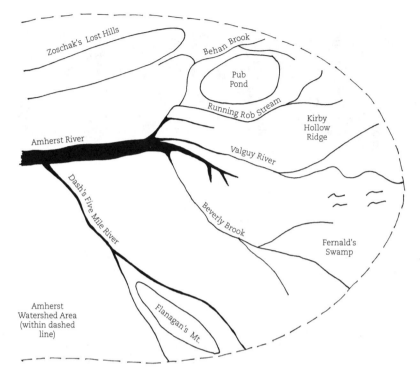

Zoschak's Lost Hills

Behan Brook

Pub Pond

Running Rob Stream

Kirby Hollow Ridge

Amherst River

Valguy River

Dash's Five Mile River

Beverly Brook

Fernald's Swamp

Amherst Watershed Area (within dashed line)

Flanagan's Mt.

A watershed acts like a drainage basin for a stream, river, lake, or reservoir.

intact in the environment for decades or longer. Plastic pollution can harm or kill wildlife (see Chapter 1).

three Rs We all know about the original version of the three Rs, but do you know the environmental version? The environmental version is reduce, reuse, and recycle. Less litter will be produced and improperly disposed of if people reduce what they use. How can they do that? By reusing what they already use. What should be done with an item when it can no longer be used? It should be recycled.

The 3 Environmental R's
Reduce Reuse Recycle

Things you can do

You can do many things to help reduce waste and fight litter. Try some of the following ideas and activities on your own or with friends and classmates. Some of these activities mention organizations to write to, or you can contact some of the organizations in Appendix A for more information. Another way to get information is to check with recycling centers or companies in your area.

Living green

Don't litter. It looks terrible. A littered sidewalk or country road shows a lack of respect for our environment and ourselves. Litter pollutes the land and the sea and can be dangerous and even deadly to wildlife.

Living green

Pick up litter and dispose of it properly. Each time it rains, water from the streets collects litter, as well as motor oil and gasoline, pet wastes, cigarette butts, and countless other pollutants. All this waste can go directly into a stream, river, pond, or lake, or it might pass into a storm drain system. Either way, it ends up in a body of water. There it can be mistaken for food by a bird, which will choke, or entangle a marine animal, which will starve.

Activity

Participate in a storm drain stenciling project in which you and your friends apply messages on or near storm drains. These messages remind people that what goes down a storm drain often ends up in water, harming or killing animals. During these projects, you need to get permission from proper authorities, gather community support from citizens and businesses, and have fun at a stenciling party. To receive information about how to create a storm drain stenciling project, contact Storm Drain

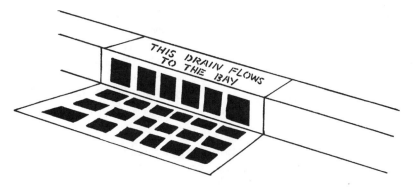

A storm drain stenciling party is a great way to get involved in protecting our environment.

Stenciling Program, The Center for Marine Conservation, 306A Buckroe Avenue, Hampton, Virginia 23664.

Bare facts

- Americans throw out about $400 million worth of aluminum every year. America must import almost all of this aluminum. If these cans were recycled, this aluminum could be back in your hands in another aluminum can in about six weeks.
- One Sunday edition of the *New York Times* uses 62,000 trees. About 10% of the paper used to print the newspaper is recycled paper.
- Using recycled crushed glass (called *cullet*) reduces the amount of energy needed to create new glass by 50 percent.

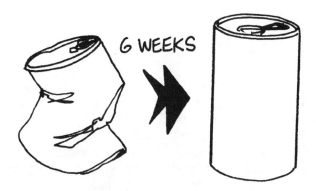

Used aluminum cans can be recycled back into new cans in as little as six weeks.

Living green When making purchases, look for items that will last a long time. Use cloth, glass, and wood whenever possible because they will decompose once they are thrown away. If you use plastic, use it over and over again as many times as is possible. For example, use a plastic grocery bag three or four times and then use it as a garbage can liner. Some grocery stores collect their plastic bags for recycling.

Living green Reuse a product as many times as possible before recycling or disposing of it. A drinking glass or ceramic mug can be used thousands of times, but a polystyrene foam cup is used for one drink before becoming garbage or litter. A cloth towel cleans up countless spills, but paper towels are used just once before becoming garbage.

A glass or a ceramic mug can be used thousands of times, but a foam or paper cup is used once and thrown away.

Activity Discuss the three environmental Rs with your friends and classmates. How can they follow the three Rs, and how much of a difference can it make? What if everyone in your class agreed to use the same lunch bag for two weeks instead of throwing them out each day? How much plastic foam would not be thrown into landfills if everyone in your class got their parents or teachers to start using ceramic mugs instead of foam cups?

Activity Recycle aluminum cans. About 50 percent of all aluminum cans are recycled. Participate in your community's aluminum recycling program if it has one. If it doesn't, try to get one started. In the meantime, find out where your local aluminum recycling facility is located and use it. Urge others in your school or community to do the same.

Recycle glass bottles. Americans throw out 28 billion bottles every year. Recycling glass helps keep it off our roads and countryside, off the beaches, out of ponds, lakes, rivers, streams, and oceans. Old glass bottles are ground up into fine particles called cullet and used to make new glass bottles.

Living green

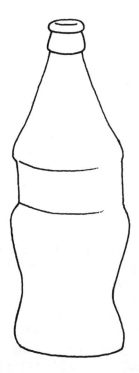

Glass bottles can be recycled into new glass containers.

Your community probably already has a glass recycling program. Participate in it and urge your friends and neighbors to do the same. If it doesn't, find out where the nearest glass recycling plant is located and use it. Urge your school administrators or community officials to begin an official glass recycling program.

Activity

Living green   Recycle paper products and use paper made from post-consumer waste. *Post-consumer* means the paper has already been used in a consumer product. For example, writing paper can be recycled into toilet paper. More recycled paper means less paper litter. It also means fewer trees need be cut down, resulting in less soil erosion.

Activity   Go to a stationery or office-supply store and look at the labels on all the boxes of paper. See how many of them state the amount of post-consumer waste used. What other labels are used? Are any of them misleading? Investigate the many different recycling logos and what they mean. Are they useful or misleading?

When buying paper products, always look for the amount of "post-consumer" waste used to make the paper. The more the better.

Activity   Start a recycling program in your school or ask your parents to recycle in their place of work. A typical American office worker uses hundreds of disposable cups each year. Use long-lasting mugs and reduce the use of foam or paper cups. Have spoons available instead of plastic or wood stirrers. Have a cloth available instead of paper towels. Reuse circulating envelopes over and over again. Recycle packing material over and over again. Not only will all these ideas help keep the environment clean, but they will also save money.

Activity   Start your own recycling management program. If your town does not have a formal recycling program for glass bottles, aluminum cans, plastic bottles, and paper products, consider starting your own in-house program. Locate the nearest recycling facility. Place a few sturdy boxes in your kitchen to accommodate about one week's worth of bottles and paper.

Label each container. After you use each bottle, rinse it and place it in the proper container. Pile the newspapers up in the box and tie it off when the bundle is about 6 inches high. Each week take them to a local recycling facility.

On the average, every person in the United States throws out about three pounds of garbage per day. Each year, Americans throw out 160 million tons of garbage. Most of this garbage ends up in landfills; the remainder is burned (*incinerated*). Although landfills and incinerators are important to our society, they both cause environmental problems. Landfills are known to leak and poison the groundwater below them. About half of all Americans depend on groundwater to provide their drinking water. Incinerators cause air pollution and leave a poisonous ash that must be disposed of in a landfill.

One of the best and simplest ways to help solve these problems is to reduce and reuse as many products as possible. For example, how many of your teachers or other adults that you know use foam cups instead of a drinking glass or ceramic mug? A foam or paper cup is used for one cup of coffee or tea and then thrown in a garbage container. A drinking glass or ceramic mug can be used for countless cups of coffee over many years. How many disposable (foam or paper) cups are used each year in your school or at your parents' place of work? How much waste could be reduced in a landfill or in an incinerator per year if everyone at that location reused their cups? After you select the location, decide what your hypothesis is.

Materials list

- A group of at least 10 adults who work at one location and routinely drink a hot beverage at a single location such as a coffee or dining room. All of the participating adults must agree to help you with this experiment. (It would be best if you could get three groups of at least 10 people each at three different locations.)
- A few large, clean garbage cans with plastic liners to collect disposable cups.
- Markers to mark the garbage cans.
- A calculator.

Label each garbage can clearly so that people know they are to be used for only disposable (foam and paper) cups.

Procedures Speak to each person who will participate in the experiment. Find out how many of them always use disposable cups and how many use reusable cups. Tell them to do everything as they usually do except to place all disposable cups in a designated garbage can. Be sure to clearly label this garbage can so they know where to throw the cups. Ask others to place no other garbage in this can.

At the end of each day, remove the plastic liner containing the cups and reline the garbage can. Count the number of cups in the container that day. Replace the bag and count the cups every day for at least two weeks, preferably one month, for each of the locations.

Conclusions At the end of the last day, add up the number of disposable cups for each location. Calculate the average number of cups thrown away by each person who used disposable cups. For example, if five people used disposable cups, and you counted 100 cups total for a week, each person threw out 20 cups a week, on the average.

Next, figure out how many cups are thrown out each year by one person at that location. In our example, that would be 50 weeks (allowing two weeks for vacation) times 20 cups per week, for a total of 1,000 cups per person per year. Figure out how many cups would be thrown out by everyone working in the building or in your school district. For example, if 100 people work in the building, and you assume half of all these people use disposable cups (remember we said five out of the 10 in our example sample), then 50 people would be throwing out 1,000 cups per week (50 people times 20 cups per week). In that building or school district, 50,000 cups (50 weeks times 1,000 cups) are thrown out each year.

Finally, figure out the weight of all these cups being placed in landfills or being incinerated. Weigh 10 cups and divide the weight by 10 to get the weight of one cup. Then multiply that weight by the total number of cups. Was your hypothesis correct? How much of a difference would it make if 10 percent of the disposable cup users changed over to reusable cups for one year? How about if half changed? How would this affect our landfills? How would it affect our litter problems?

Our polluted beaches & coastlines

MORE THAN 50 percent of the U.S. population lives within 100 miles of a coast. It's no surprise that the most polluted waters are found just offshore. Coastal cities destroy habitats where marine organisms live. Plastic waste and garbage litter many beaches and overwhelm some coastal areas. Sewage treatment outflow pipes dump pollutants into many coastal waters. Mud dredged up from harbors and channels containing toxic materials are dumped into less-traveled waters. Offshore drilling generates waste materials containing toxic substances that are often dumped into the sea. Oil leaks are not uncommon.

Treated industrial wastes often flows directly into bodies of water.

Terms to know   **coastal zone** Marine habitats can be divided into those found in the open ocean, called the *ocean zone*, and those found along the coast, called the *coastal zone*. The coastal zone includes all the water above the continental shelf. This zone begins at the shore and can go out to sea several hundred miles in some areas.

The coastal zone contains some of the most important environments on earth. They are home to many fish, clams, oysters, crabs, sponges, anemones, and jellyfish, among others. In much of this water, the sunlight penetrates to the bottom, allowing plants to attach to the floor below, providing shelter for many other organisms. These areas have a great deal of variety in their types of ecosystems, because there are many types of shorelines. Rocky shores have very different ecosystems from sandy shores. The coastal zone has many unique, important habitats, including estuaries, coastal wetlands, and coral reefs.

Coastal waters are rich in sea life.

coastal wetlands Land that is flooded for all or part of the year is called a *wetland*. If it contains salt water, it is called a *coastal wetland* (as opposed to a freshwater, inland wetland). Coastal wetlands include bays, lagoons, and salt marshes. These wetlands all have grasses as the most common type of vegetation. In very warm regions, however, coastal wetlands are primarily swamps inhabited by mangrove trees.

estuary An estuary is a coastal ecosystem in which fresh water from a river mixes with salt water from the sea. This mixing of fresh and salt water produces brackish waters. Since the amount of salt, temperature, and other factors varies with the tides, only certain kinds of organisms with wide tolerance ranges can inhabit this type of ecosystem. Estuaries are among the most productive ecosystems on earth, since the constant flow of water from the river into the estuary provides high concentrations of nutrients, which allows these organisms to thrive. In the United States, 55 percent of all estuaries and coastal wetlands have been damaged or totally destroyed.

human impact on estuaries and coastal wetlands Estuaries and coastal wetlands were thought until recently to be worthless, mosquito-infested regions. Many of these areas were used as dumping grounds for waste, while others have been drained, filled in, and built on, and still others have had their source waters diverted for human use.

In fact, estuaries, swamps, and marshes are one of the most important of all habitats. These regions are spawning and nursing grounds for 70 percent of U.S. commercial fish and shellfish, and they are the breeding grounds and habitats for waterfowl and other wildlife. They filter out and dilute pollutants from the rivers and streams that feed them before the water reaches the sea. They also protect inland areas from storm waves and absorb large amounts of water that would otherwise cause flooding.

coral reef Marine ecosystems along the coastal zone contain many unique habitats, such as coral reefs. Coral reefs are found

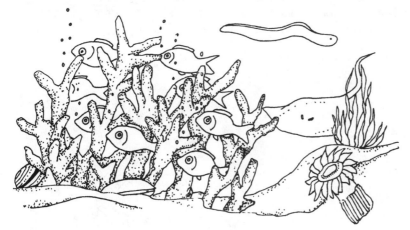

The numbers and variety of organisms found in coral reefs are similar to that of tropical rain forests.

in warm regions of our planet. A coral reef is built primarily by tiny *coelenterates*, which are cylindrical in shape with a pouch-like mouth surrounded by tentacles that capture prey and bring it into the mouth. (Sea anemones and jellyfish are other types of coelenterates.)

These organisms attach themselves to the sea floor. They release calcium, which acts as a foundation for other individuals. As the amount of calcium increases, large coral reefs are formed. Only the surface of the reef contains live coral organisms. The rest is just the remaining calcium. Thousands of species of fish and other organisms, such as sea urchins, feed on the algae, bacteria, and other microorganisms that live in coral reef ecosystems.

Things you can do

You can do many things to help protect our beaches and coastal marine life. Try some of the following ideas and activities on your own or with friends and classmates. Some of these activities mention organizations to write to, or you can contact some of the organizations in Appendix A for more information.

Living green

Carry a waste disposal bag with you on the beach. How many times have you seen overflowing garbage cans at parks or beaches? If a beach does not have enough refuse containers, speak with beach officials about getting more or increasing the number and frequency of pick-ups.

Living green

Urge your local beach or shore officials to provide recycling containers at the beach. Speak with these officials about their

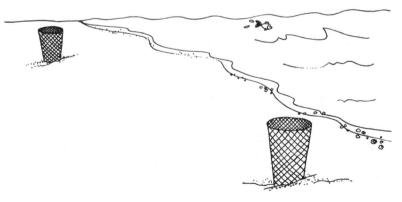

Garbage containers are an important way to help protect marine animals.

recycling policies. Litter in the ocean looks like food to many sea animals. When an animal tries to eat litter, it often chokes or has its food passageway blocked so that it starves to death. Marine mammals become entangled in plastic rings and wrappers.

Participate in or begin your own adopt-a-beach project. These projects get everyone in a community involved. They promote environmental awareness and stewardship. To begin such a program, identify the beach to protect and then determine whether such a program already exists by speaking with the beach manager. If it does exist, contact the coordinator of the program. If not, start one. For information about starting your own adopt-a-beach program, contact the California Coastal Commission, 45 Fremont Street, Suite 2000, San Francisco, California 94105.

Activity

On September 20, 1986, 2,800 volunteers participated in the Texas coastal cleanup organized by Linda Maraniss and the Center for Marine Conservation. Volunteers filled 8,000 trash bags with marine debris collected on only 120 miles of Texas beach. By 1988, this event became national, and by 1993, more than 160,000 volunteers participated in 32 countries to clean up more than 5,000 miles of coastline. They collected more than 3.5 million pounds of debris.

Bare facts

Participate in the International Coastal Cleanup. On the third Saturday in September each year, the Center for Marine Conservation coordinates the largest volunteer cleanup in the world to eliminate marine debris on a global level. During this event, coastal debris is collected, identified, and weighed. The data about this debris has been used to pass important laws to protect our oceans.

Activity

To participate in this event, contact the Center for Marine Conservation, Atlantic Coast Office, 1725 DeSales Street, NW, Suite 500, Washington, D.C. 20036, or the Pacific Coast Office, 580 Market Street, Suite 550, San Francisco, California 94104.

5TH ANNUAL
COUNTY COASTAL CLEANUP
APRIL 4th

HELP CLEAN UP OUR BEACHES
PUNCH OUT PLASTIC POLLUTION

TO SIGN UP
call 123-4567

Participating in a coastal cleanup day is a great way to get involved.

Activity Have your class write to your elected officials asking them to support the continuation and strengthening of the Coastal Zone Management Act. This act is responsible for the management of coastal development and conservation. For more information contact the Coast Alliance, 235 Pennsylvania Avenue, SE, Washington, D.C. 20003.

Living green Adopt a marine animal. Many marine animals are being forced into extinction by human activities, including habitat destruction caused by dams, construction, and agriculture. We also release poisons in the form of pesticides and toxic chemicals into the environment, which kills marine life. Many zoos and aquariums help save certain species from extinction. Some of them let you participate by adopting an animal. When people donate money, it is used to care for a specific marine animal. For more information, contact the American Association of Zoological Parks and Aquariums, Oglebay Park, Wheeling, West Virginia 26003.

Many organizations let you adopt an animal.

Living green

Don't buy coral. Coral is a popular souvenir item. Coral reefs are one of the most productive ecosystems on our planet (see "Terms to Know" at the beginning of this chapter). They rival tropical rain forests when it comes to biodiversity. They are also one of the most fragile ecosystems on earth. Many countries have banned the collection, sale, and export of coral.

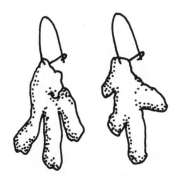

One way to help protect endangered animals and sensitive ecosystems is to not buy products made from those organisms or habitats. Coral earrings and exotic leather goods are examples.

Living green

If you find a beached whale or dolphin, get an adult to help you and follow these steps:

1. Prevent a crowd of people from circling the animal, and keep dogs and other pets away.
2. Observe the animal from a distance.

3. Note the physical characteristics, such as size and color, since this information can help an expert identify the animal.

4. Note the physical condition of the animal. Does the animal look sick or have wounds?

5. Look for a tag of some sort.

6. Determine the animal's exact location, so qualified help can locate the animal.

7. Call the Marine Mammal Center at (415) 289-7325 or the Marine Animal Resource Center at (206) 285-SEAL, or ask the local beach manager if a local volunteer group is available to help.

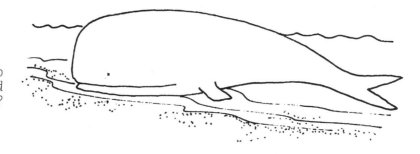

Would you know what to do if you found a beached whale or dolphin?

Activity   Have your class get together to write to your elected officials asking them to support the continuation and strengthening of the Endangered Species Act. This act identifies endangered and threatened species, identifies habitats important to their survival, and offers guidelines on how to protect these areas.

Living green   While fishing, look before casting to see if a seabird, for example a pelican, is close by. If so, wait until the bird has left the area. If you use a small fish for bait on a hook, the bird might try to eat the fish and swallow the hook.

Living green   Don't feed pelicans or other seabirds in an area where people are fishing. One of the major causes of injury and death to seabirds are fish hooks and fishing lines.

Never fish near a seabird such as a pelican. It might swallow your hook while trying to eat your bait.

Never throw a monofilament fishing line or net in the water. These lines and nets are not biodegradable and can entangle and kill countless fish or marine animals.

Living green

Adopt a seabird. Help save injured seabirds by joining an adopt-a-bird program. For more information, contact the Suncoast Seabird Sanctuary, 18328 Gulf Boulevard, Indian Shores, Florida 34635.

Living green

Have your class write letters to ask your elected officials to support the continuation and strengthening of the National Marine Sanctuaries Act. This act is the only federal law designed to protect ocean life.

Activity

Although nutrient enrichment might at first glance sound like something good happening to the environment, it is not. Ecosystems like a pond strike a balance between the amount of nutrients entering the pond and the amount used by the organisms in that pond.

Science project: Nutrient enrichment
Project overview

When people change the amount of nutrients that go into a pond or other ecosystem, the balance is lost and the natural order is destroyed. People change the amount of nutrients entering ponds and other aquatic ecosystems in many ways, but sewage from cities is the main cause.

Most of your waste products are washed down the sink, toilet, or drain pipe. From there, waste enters a water treatment plant to be cleaned before it is released back into the environment.

Some detergents contain phosphates, which are not removed by most sewage treatment plants before water is released back into the environment.

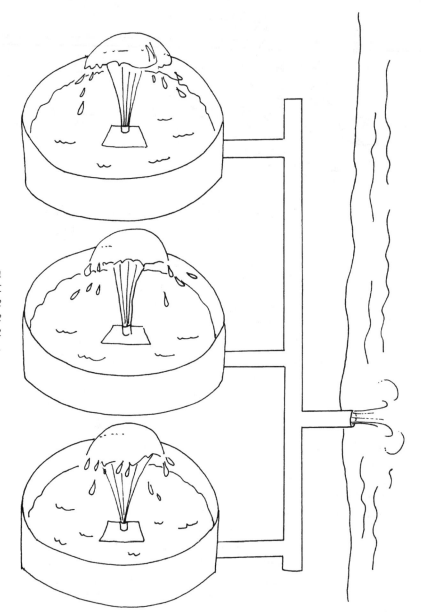

After the water has passed through the treatment plant, it is released back into the environment, but it is not as clean as it once was. It often contains large amounts of nutrients such as phosphates from detergents. Adding even small amounts of phosphorus to a pond can have a serious effect.

During this project you will see what happens to pond water when detergent phosphates are added to the water. What effect will nutrient enrichment have on pond water, if any? What is your hypothesis? This project must be done under the direct supervision of your teacher.

Materials list

- A potassium phosphate solution. This solution can be made in the laboratory by your teacher, or it can be purchased from a biological supply house (Appendix B).
- A quart jar with a lid to collect a water sample from the pond.
- 8 clear containers such as plastic cups or drinking glasses.
- Marker or labels to identify each container.
- An eyedropper.
- Paper towels.
- Access to a pond or lake to collect water samples.

Procedures

Fill the quart jar with water from the pond. Label the jar with the location. Bring the jar back to your school or home. Label a set of plastic cups with the numbers 1 through 8. Fill each cup halfway with the pond water. For cups 1 and 2, add nothing—they will be the control group. For cups 3 and 4, add 2 drops of the phosphate solution. To cups 5 and 6, add 4 drops of the phosphate solution. To cups 7 and 8, add 8 drops of the solution.

Once all the cups are ready, place a paper towel over the top of each cup and place them all in a sunny part of the room. All of the cups must receive the same amount of light. Make observations about the cups. Write down the appearance of the water in each cup, such as "light" or "dark green color" or "very cloudy." Each day for 10 days, add the same number of drops as you did initially into each cup. Continue to write down your observations.

Conclusions How did the phosphates affect the pond water? What did you notice in the water? Did the different groups containing different amounts of phosphate appear different in the beginning of the project? How about at the end of the project? What do you think is happening in the water? How might this change affect a natural pond or lake?

The open sea

EARTH IS called the water planet, and for good reason. It is estimated that the total amount of water on, in, and around our planet is 360 billion billion gallons. Water covers more than 70 percent of the earth's surface. Oceans are home to roughly 250,000 species.

Since almost all water runs to the sea, any form of pollution stands a good chance of ending up in the ocean. Water pollution is caused by many different things. Sewage from our homes and businesses and chemicals added to the water by industries make their way to the sea.

Fertilizers and pesticides run off the land with the rains and poison the sea. Many other products, such as gasoline and plastics, make their way into bodies of water. Plastic products are like floating time bombs at sea, waiting to entangle or choke a fish or marine animal. Soil erosion causes large amounts of sediment to enter bodies of water, which damages or destroys aquatic ecosystems.

During the past 20 years, more than 350 oil-carrying vessels have sunk worldwide. Even small losses of oil can have drastic effects on the local ecosystem. Oil globules spilled from ships have been found from the Antarctic to the Bering Sea.

Oil spills big and small cause a great deal of environmental harm.

Terms to know

marine ecosystems The regions of the ocean can most easily be described by their distance from the shore. The region within a few miles of shore is called the *coastal zone*, while the water beyond is the *ocean zone*. The most productive marine ecosystems are found in the coastal zone. The study of marine ecosystems is called *oceanography*.

MARPOL MARPOL is an abbreviation for marine pollution. It refers to an international law signed by the United States and many other nations. A portion of this law, called Annex V, regulates ocean dumping and bans dumping plastics anywhere at sea.

MARPOL, which stands for marine pollution, is one of the most important laws protecting the marine environment.

It is illegal for any vessel to dump plastic trash anywhere in the ocean or navigable waters of the United States. Annex V of the MARPOL TREATY is a new International Law for a cleaner, safer marine environment. Each violation of these requirements may result in civil penalty up to $25,000, a fine up to $500,000, and imprisonment up to 6 years.

U.S. Lakes, Rivers, Bays, Sounds and 3 miles from shore
ILLEGAL TO DUMP
Plastic and Garbage
Paper   Metal
Rags   Crockery
Glass   Dunnage
Food

3 to 12 miles
ILLEGAL TO DUMP
Plastic
Dunnage (lining and packing materials that float) also if not ground to less than one inch:
Paper   Crockery
Rags   Metal
Glass   Food

12 to 25 miles
ILLEGAL TO DUMP
Plastic
Dunnage (lining and packing materials that float)

Outside 25 miles
ILLEGAL TO DUMP
Plastic

State and local regulations may further restrict the disposal of garbage.

Working Together, We Can All Make A Difference!
Center for Marine Conservation   1725 DeSales Street, NW Washington, DC 20036 (202) 429-5609

Things you can do

You can do many things to help reduce pollution at sea when you go boating or on a cruise. Try some of the following ideas and activities if your family or a friend's family owns a boat. Some of these activities mention organizations to write to, or you can contact some of the organizations in Appendix A for more information.

Keep a garbage can onboard and be sure everyone uses it. Don't let anyone throw cigarette butts overboard—marine life often mistakes them for food. Never allow plastic products to be thrown overboard. They are threats to marine life and take decades to decompose. Don't discard old fishing lines or nets overboard because they can entangle marine life for years to come. Save all garbage for the marina.

Living green

Have a "Stow-It, Don't Throw-It" party to improve awareness about the dangers of marine litter among sport fishers. This project consists of two parts. First you provide marine debris educational literature to all participants; then you hold a garbage-bag return raffle and award prizes.

Activity

For more information about this project, contact the Stow-It, Don't Throw-It! Program, The Center for Marine Conservation, 1725 DeSales Street, NW, #500, Washington, D.C. 20036.

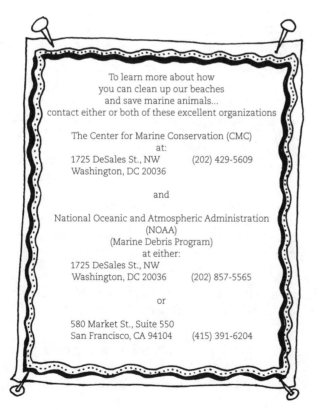

To learn more about how
you can clean up our beaches
and save marine animals...
contact either or both of these excellent organizations

The Center for Marine Conservation (CMC)
at:
1725 DeSales St., NW   (202) 429-5609
Washington, DC 20036

and

National Oceanic and Atmospheric Administration
(NOAA)
(Marine Debris Program)
at either:
1725 DeSales St., NW
Washington, DC 20036   (202) 857-5565

or

580 Market St., Suite 550
San Francisco, CA 94104   (415) 391-6204

The Center for Marine Conservation in Washington, D.C., has many outstanding programs for young people.

Activity Hold a "Pier Pressure" event to increase awareness among recreational boaters about the hazards of marine litter. This project encourages boaters to act responsibly about marine debris by helping them become informed and by peer pressure. Organizers spread out to cover a pier, educate the boaters, pass out free literature, and hand out a placard describing MARPOL laws (see "Terms to Know").

Everyone gets a garbage bag to return to the marina for proper disposal. For complete information about the Pier Pressure program, contact the Center for Marine Conservation. You can find the address on page 69.

Living green Support green marinas. The National Marine Manufacturers Association has established an award to promote environmentally sound boating facilities. Urge your marina manager to get involved in protecting our oceans.

Marinas contribute to marine pollution. Marinas that try to prevent marine pollution are called green marinas.

Living green If your family's boat has a toilet installed onboard, be sure to use the nearest sewage pump-out facility instead of discharging the waste into the water. If you use a portable toilet, don't discharge at sea.

Living green Report any marina that does not adhere to MARPOL regulations. Notify local Coast Guard authorities.

Living green Be careful to not spill fuel when you're filling up your fuel tank. Most marine pumps don't have automatic shut-off valves like automobile gas pumps do. Many aftermarket devices are

Every time a boater says "fill 'er up," there is a risk of spilling gasoline into the water.

available that make it easier to prevent gas spills during fill-ups. Check with your marine supplier and urge that these devices be used at marinas.

If you know someone thinking about buying a small boat, have them consider a four-cycle motor or one of the new electric outboard motors that offer pollution-free power. The most common source of fuel contamination isn't spills, but two-cycle outboard motors, which release oil into the water with the exhaust.

Living green

People are outraged when they hear about major oil spills like the Exxon *Valdez* incident. These spills, however, account for only 12 percent of the oil spilled into the sea each year. Most of the remaining 88 percent comes from normal commercial shipping operations and recreational boaters.

Bare facts

Be sure the motor on your boat doesn't leak oil or gas into the water or drain fluids into the water.

Living green

Place a bilge pillow (an oil-absorbing sponge) in your bilge to remove oil and reduce the risk of a spill.

Living green

Minimize your use of toxic chemicals. Nontoxic does not mean noneffective. Most marine stores carry a full line of nontoxic products for the bilge, holding tank, and for cleaning boats.

Living green

Living green   Don't use paints containing chemicals such as TBT (tributyltin) to control the growth of barnacles, seaweeds, and other marine organisms on the hull of your vessel. These paints are poisonous to marine life. Use new environmentally safe marine paints that contain silicon or Teflon. These paints make the surface slick, which prevents growth. Other environmentally safe marine paints are hard paints that last a long time but won't be absorbed into the water. For more information contact your local marina or the Puget Sound Alliance, 130 Nickerson, Suite 107, Seattle, Washington 98109.

Most marine paints contain poisonous chemicals to keep organisms from growing on the hulls of boats.

Living green   Don't use liquid detergents to disperse oil in the bilge or directly in the water. Detergents do not get rid of the oil (they just make the droplets smaller, which can be even more harmful to marine life), and the soap itself is harmful.

Living green   Don't use detergents containing phosphorus when cleaning your vessel. They are harmful to aquatic ecosystems.

Most cleaning products sold are toxic (poisonous) to marine life, but other marine cleaning products are environmentally safe. Here are some examples:

- Replace bleach with borax or hydrogen peroxide.
- Replace scouring powders with baking soda.
- Replace floor cleaners with one cup of white wine vinegar to each quart of warm water.
- Replace a general cleaner with bicarbonate of soda and vinegar.
- Replace a head cleaner with baking soda and a heavy brush.
- Replace brass cleaner with Worcestershire sauce.
- Replace copper cleaner with lemon juice and salt.
- Replace fiberglass cleaner with baking soda paste.
- Replace indoor wood cleaner with almond or olive oil.

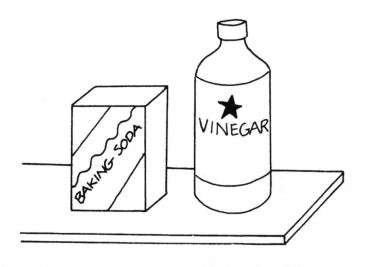

Many household products can be used to make safe cleaning fluids.

Buy only what you need and plan to use so you won't have to dispose of leftovers. If you have leftover chemicals or paints, don't dispose of them. See if a neighbor can use them.

Living green

Recycle your used oil, filters, paints, and batteries. Find out where your local recycling center is located and use it.

Living green

Living green   When painting or cleaning a boat while it is out of the water, use tarps or paper to keep paint chips, debris, and cleaners out of the water.

Living green   Stay at least 100 yards away from seabirds and marine mammals that are nesting or caring for their young. In some situations the presence of people can cause a mother to abandon her young.

Don't steer your boat too close to seabirds or other marine life.

Living green   Obey posted marine speed limits. In sensitive environments, a 2-knot increase over the posted limit can damage beaches, coastal banks, and wetlands.

Living green   Avoid areas where bottom sea grasses grow. They hold sediment and provide a home for marine life. These areas are too fragile and important to destroy.

Living green   If anyone you know is going on a cruise, encourage them to look for illegal dumping of plastic waste at sea. There is a worldwide ban on the dumping of any kind of plastic in the open sea and navigable waterways. (See "Terms to Know" on MARPOL.) It is illegal to dump plastic anywhere at sea. In the near future, it will be illegal to dump any and all trash in the Caribbean Sea, around the Bahamas, and in the Gulf of Mexico.

Keep these facts in mind if you see any dumping. If the ship owners are convicted and fined, the person who reported it might receive a large reward. Tell anyone going on a cruise to bring a video camera and to look for illegal dumping.

Inform your parents and other adults about illegal dumping at sea and ask them to report it if they witness it. Illegal dumping usually takes place at night when passengers are asleep. Try to have at least two additional witnesses and get videos or pictures of the actual event. Also try to get a "fix" on the ship's position at that time and photograph any landmarks.

As soon as you enter port, contact the Coast Guard Marine Safety Office or the Coast Guard captain of the port. The phone number will be in the blue pages of the phone book. Ask to speak with the officer in charge of MARPOL violations. For more information, contact NOAA's Marine Debris Information Office, c/o the Center for Marine Conservation. (See Appendix A for the address.)

It is illegal to dump garbage at sea.

While traveling, be careful what you buy as souvenirs. Don't buy watchbands, handbags, belts, or shoes made of reptile skins or leathers. Crocodile skin items and sea turtle items are especially popular. Remember what had to be killed to create these items. Is it worth it? Is it necessary?

Living green

Exotic leather bags, belts, and shoes are popular. Find out what kind of animal was killed to produce the product before buying it.

Science project: Toxic paints
Project overview

Marine paints usually contain poisonous chemicals. These chemicals are mixed into the paints to prevent algae and other organisms from growing on the painted surface. Recreational boats and commercial, military, and cruise ships all use these environmentally dangerous paints to keep things from growing on their hulls.

Unfortunately, many of the chemicals used in these paints don't kill only the organisms that could grow on the hulls, they also kill many types of marine plants and animals as well. Some of these paints have been banned; others have restricted uses.

A new type of marine paint is being sold with hopes that it can do its job yet not be harmful to the environment. But do these new environmentally safe products work as well as the older paints? How do different types of marine paints compare in their ability to reduce algae growth? What is your hypothesis? This project should only be performed under the supervision of an adult.

Materials list

- Six 1-pint mason jars.
- Pond water from a local pond.
- A few desk lamps.
- Marker.
- Paper towels.
- 2 small model plane paintbrushes.
- Microscope, microscope slides, and coverslips

- One standard marine paint (called *anti-fouling paint*) containing poisonous chemicals and one new type that does not. You need a very small quantity of each. Use white paint only. Speak with a knowledgeable person in a marina supply store for assistance in getting the paint.

Fill each mason jar about three-quarters full of pond water. Leave all the jars under a desk lamp for seven days. Don't keep the lamp too close to the jars or the water will overheat, killing the microbes. Add more water as the water level drops. After a week, you should have a rich growth of microbes in the mason jars. If the jars are not greenish in color, add more pond or aquarium water and wait another few days. You must see algae growth (the water should have a greenish tinge) in or on the mason jars before continuing.

Procedures

Use the first small paintbrush to apply a thin coat of the standard marine paint to one side of a microscope slide. Paint two slides.

Use the model plane paintbrush to apply the marine paint to one side of the microscope slide.

Next paint two other slides, using the environmentally safe paint. Label the slides so you can tell which is which. Be sure to use a different brush for each paint to be tested. Let all the slides air dry for two days. Be sure to keep them outside, since most paints give off dangerous fumes.

Carefully place one slide in each prepared mason jar. The painted sides of the slides should face up in the water. Label each jar with the type of paint it contains. Put two unpainted slides in the remaining jars to act as controls. Leave all the slides in the jars for 14 days. During this period, add water to the jars to keep the slides under water. Keep the jars under the lamps or in a sunny area.

At the end of two weeks, remove all the slides. Be sure the labels are still visible on each slide. Wipe the unpainted side of the slides clean with paper towels. (For the control slides, wipe one side of the slides clean.) Place the coverslips over the sides of the slides you did not wipe clean. Observe the slides under a microscope. You'll have to increase the amount of light passing through the condenser of the scope, since the slides have paint on them; you might need an additional light source.

Conclusions Did algae grow on all the slides? Did you notice a difference between the controls and the painted slides? Did the same amount grow on all the slides, or did one of the paints reduce or prevent growth better than the other? Does it appear that some of the new environmentally safe marine paints are as good at preventing hull growth as the traditional toxic paints?

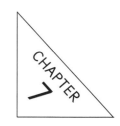

Threats to marine life

POLLUTION and the destruction of habitats are threatening many species of marine life. Overharvesting the seas with driftnets, gill nets, shrimp trawlers, and factory ships are destroying entire communities of marine life. This chapter tells you some ways you can help protect marine life.

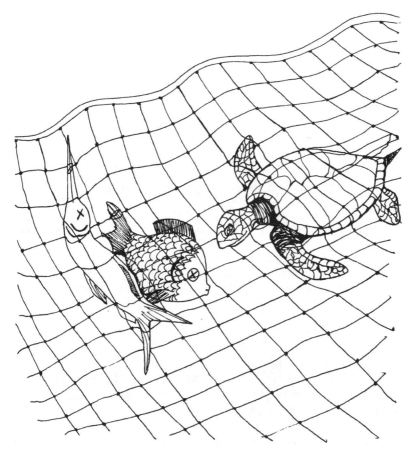

Driftnets act like walls of death in the sea.

Threats to marine life   79

Terms to know

Marine Mammal Protection Act This act became a U.S. law in 1972. Its purpose is to protect marine mammals, including dolphins, whales, and sea otters, among others, in U.S. waters. It contains regulations regarding the use of purse seine nets, driftnets, and gill nets.

turtle excluder device (TED) Shrimp trawlers in the Gulf of Mexico and off the southeastern shore of the United States accidentally trap more than 45,000 sea turtles each year in their long cone-shaped shrimp nets. More than 10,000 of these turtles die of suffocation because they are trapped beneath the water for long periods of time. New laws in the United States require the use of turtle excluder devices (TEDs), which allow almost all of these creatures to escape from the net without releasing the shrimp.

TED releases
sea turtles, but shrimp pass
through and are caught

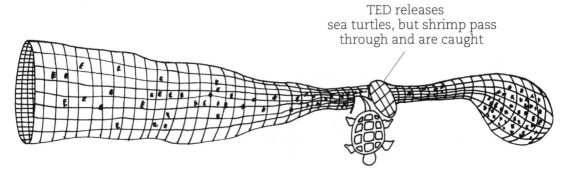

The turtle excluder device (TED) saves and releases sea turtles from shrimp trawler nets.

A TED is a metal or nylon grid inserted into the middle portion of the cone-shaped net. The grid allows shrimp to pass through and remain netted, but large animals, such as sea turtles, bump into the grid and are stopped. The grid is placed at an angle so the turtles slide toward the side of the net and are released through an opening.

driftnet A driftnet is a fishing device used to catch large numbers of tuna, salmon, and squid in a short period of time. In addition to the intended catch, driftnets entangle many fish and other marine life that the fishers are not interested in. This unwanted catch is called *bycatch*. The bycatch includes dolphins, sharks, whales, marine turtles, and seabirds. The bycatch is thrown back into the sea, but most of the creatures are usually dead or dying. Driftnets have reduced the commercial fishing harvest and destroyed marine ecosystems in many parts of our oceans.

Driftnets are finely woven nylon mesh nets up to 50 miles in length that drop into deep waters about 40 feet down. As unsuspecting fish swim into these huge walls of mesh, their gills become entangled and they suffocate. It is estimated that 2,500 ships put out over 50,000 miles of driftnets and their coastal water equivalent, *gill nets*, every night. Hundreds of miles of these nets become entangled or lost at sea each year, where they continue to trap countless fish and marine mammals.

purse seine net A purse seine net is a fishing device used to catch large numbers of tuna. During the 1950s, tuna fishers discovered that yellowfin tuna are often found swimming below dolphin herds. (It's believed the tuna follow dolphins because of the dolphins' ability to locate food.) Tuna boats routinely

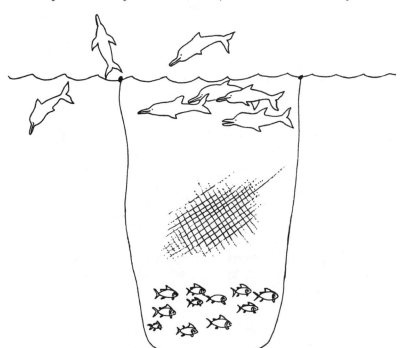

Herds of dolphin are captured along with tuna in purse seine nets.

encircle dolphin herds with purse seine nets and haul in the tuna catch below, along with the dolphins above. The dolphins usually die before being released. It's estimated that over 100,000 dolphins die in these nets each year.

Many tuna canners are now selling "dolphin-safe tuna," which means the tuna was not caught in purse seine nets or driftnets.

Things you can do

You can do many things to help to protect marine life. Try some of the following ideas and activities on your own or with friends and classmates. Some of these activities mention organizations to write to, or you can contact some of the organizations in Appendix A for more information.

Living green

Help protect sea turtles. The Sea Turtle Conservation Program and the Sea Turtle Restoration Project protect sea turtles and try to prevent trade in endangered species products. Contact the Sea Turtle Conservation Program, Center for Marine Conservation, or the Sea Turtle Restoration Project at the Earth Island Institute, 300 Broadway, Suite 28, San Francisco, California 94133.

Activity

Get your class to write to your elected officials asking them to keep the Marine Mammal Protection Act strong. This act protects all species of whales, dolphins, seals, sea lions, manatees, sea otters, and polar bears.

Living green

Help to protect seabirds. The Marine Debris and Entanglement Program tries to reduce the hazards of nylon fishing nets that entangle seabirds and other marine life. The program urges the passage of laws that prevent harmful fishing practices.

Activity

Have your class write to your elected officials asking them to support the continuation and strengthening of the Ocean Dumping Act. This act manages the disposal of all forms of waste into the oceans, including sewage sludge, industrial waste, and dredged waste.

Hundreds of thousands of marine animals die senselessly each year during commercial tuna and salmon fishing operations that use driftnets, gill nets, and purse seine nets. Since dolphins and other animals are not the intended catch, they are called bycatch. As the catch is taken in, the dead and dying animals are thrown back into the sea.

In 1990 alone, Japanese driftnet fishing boats dumped back into the ocean 39 million fish, 700,000 sharks, 270,000 seabirds, and 26,000 mammals, most of which were dead or dying, and all considered bycatch.

Don't buy tuna unless it has been certified dolphin-safe by the Earth Island Institute. Look for the Dolphin Safe Tuna logo on cans, or contact the Earth Island Institute for a list of brands. Look for pet foods that use only dolphin-safe tuna products as well. Also get the latest list of restaurant chains and food service companies that use only dolphin-safe tuna. Contact the International Marine Mammal Project, Earth Island Institute, 300 Broadway, Suite 28, San Francisco, California 94133.

Living green

Dolphin-safe tuna means the tuna was caught without endangering dolphins.

Urge your local supermarkets and restaurants to sell only dolphin-safe tuna products. Urge school authorities and your parents' places of business to serve only dolphin-safe tuna in their cafeterias.

Activity

Have your class contact your elected officials to ask them to support the International Dolphin Conservation Act of 1992. This act would drastically reduce the killing of dolphins by U.S. tuna boats and make the sale of tuna that is not dolphin-safe illegal in the United States.

Activity

Activity   Support the International Whaling Commission. During the past 100 years, hundreds of thousands of blue, sperm, humpback, and minke whales have been hunted by commercial whalers, some almost into extinction. The International Whaling Commission declared a worldwide ban on commercial whaling that officially began in 1986.

Ask your class to urge your elected officials to support this global agreement now and in the future. Contact the American Cetacean Society, P.O. Box 2639, San Pedro, California 90731. This society is the oldest whale conservation group in the world.

Activity   Write to your elected officials urging them to take a strong anti-whaling position. Learn about whales and see why there is a need to protect these amazing mammals. Although there has been a worldwide effort to stop commercial whaling, it continues to this day in some countries. One way to stop hunting whales is to help develop whale-watching programs. The money that could be made watching whales could convince some countries to stop commercial whaling operations. Contact Whales Alive, Box 2058, Kihei, Hawaii 96753.

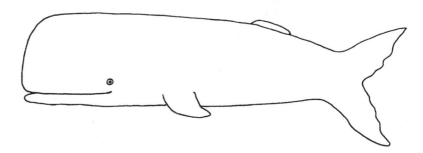

Whaling still continues today in spite of international laws that try to prevent it.

Living green   Learn more about sharks, and help teach your classmates the truth about sharks. The many myths about sharks have led to the abuse and decline in shark populations. Contact the Pelagic Shark Research Foundation (PSRF), 333 Lake Avenue, Suite H, Maritime Center, Santa Cruz, California 95062.

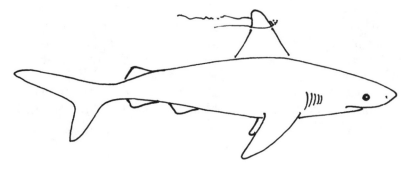

Some sharks are on the endangered species list.

Help protect endangered seals by participating in the Species Recovery Program, which works to conserve endangered seal species around the world. Seals are endangered because they have lost much of their habitat to development, they are injured or killed by boaters, they become sick from oil spills, and they get trapped in fishing nets and strangled on plastic debris. Contact the Species Recovery Program, The Center for Marine Conservation (see Appendix A for the address).

Living green

In many areas, the habitats of seals have become polluted or destroyed by development.

Science project: Dolphin-safe tuna
Project overview

As discussed previously, tens of thousands of dolphin are killed each year in purse seine nets and driftnets. Fishers haul in herds of dolphin along with tuna. Most of the captured dolphins die before being released back into the water. Many people are concerned about these needless deaths and purchase only tuna caught by methods that do not endanger dolphins. Tuna caught without harming dolphins are packaged as dolphin-safe tuna.

Most supermarkets carry many different brands of tuna.

During this project, you will determine what percentage of tuna sold in your local supermarket is dolphin-safe. You will then go on to find out what percentage of restaurants in your area serve dolphin-safe tuna. What are your hypotheses? Do you think dolphin-safe tuna is common or rare?

Materials list

- A large supermarket with a wide variety of brands of tuna and an employee willing and able to help you.
- At least 10 restaurants that serve tuna dishes and an employee willing to tell you if they use dolphin-safe tuna.

Procedures

Go to your local supermarket with a notebook. Write down all the different brands of canned tuna. Write down which ones have dolphin-safe labels and which do not. Then look at the fresh or frozen seafood section to see if they carry tuna. Write down any different brands you might see.

Frozen and fresh tuna labels do not contain as much information as canned tuna labels.

Next, find the store manager or other knowledgeable person and ask them if they can tell you roughly what the percentage is of total tuna sales for each particular brand. For example, is 75 percent of the tuna sold in the store dolphin-safe tuna? Then ask about the fresh or frozen tuna and get the same information.

Go to or call as many restaurants as possible and ask to speak with the manager. Ask if they use dolphin-safe tuna. Write down what each said and then figure out the percentage of all the restaurants that use dolphin-safe tuna.

Conclusions

Does your supermarket carry dolphin-safe tuna in cans? Is the fresh or frozen tuna dolphin-safe? What percent of the brands sold are dolphin-safe? What percentage of all the canned tuna sold in the store is dolphin-safe? How about fresh or frozen? How does canned tuna compare with fresh or frozen? Why might you find canned dolphin-safe tuna but not fresh dolphin-safe tuna? Was your hypothesis correct?

What about the restaurants? What percentage carry dolphin-safe tuna? Are restaurant managers concerned about this problem? If so, why? If not, why not? Was your hypothesis correct?

CHAPTER 8

Hazardous wastes: Polluting our planet

HAZARDOUS wastes are substances that are dangerous when they are disposed of. They can catch fire, explode, corrode metal, or cause illness. Hazardous wastes that are dangerous to the health of humans or other organisms are said to be toxic. Some of these wastes are *acutely toxic*, meaning they can make you sick immediately. Other types of hazardous wastes might take years or decades to make an organism ill. This process is called *chronic toxicity*.

Getting rid of hazardous wastes has become an environmental problem. The United States has about 250,000 hazardous waste disposal sites, all of which pose a threat to our groundwater supplies, our health, and the environment in general.

HAZARDOUS WASTE SITE
NO ADMITTANCE!

The Environmental Protection Agency's Superfund tries to clean up existing hazardous waste sites.

toxic pollution Toxic pollution is any substance found in the environment that causes harm to an organism's normal functioning. Since these substances can be found in the air, water, or soil, toxic pollution is actually a part of air, water, and

Terms to know

soil pollution. In the United States alone, millions of tons of toxic pollutants are produced and disposed of each year. The government has passed laws in response to concerns about toxic pollution, including the Resource Conservation and Recovery Act, the Toxic Substances Control Act, and the Superfund.

Toxic Substances Control Act of 1976 This law gave the EPA the authority to test new chemicals before they can be sold.

Love Canal Love Canal is a symbol of the hazardous waste problem in our country. For 10 years beginning in the late 1940s, Hooker Chemicals and Plastics Corporation dumped 22,000 tons of toxic wastes in steel drums into an old canal. In 1953, the company placed topsoil over the site containing the drums and turned the property over to the Niagara Falls School District. A school, recreational fields, and almost 1,000 homes were built on the site over the next few years.

Beginning in 1976, residents began to notice odd smells and found that children playing around the canal often received chemical burns. The drums were leaking toxic wastes into the sewers, lawns, and even basements of homes near the site. Concerned citizens, including Lois Gibbs, performed informal health studies that revealed high numbers of many types of disorders. The publicity generated by concerned citizens forced the state to perform formal health studies, and in 1978, the state closed the school and relocated some of the residents living closest to the canal. More than 700 remaining residents finally convinced the federal government to declare the entire area a disaster area. As a result, almost all the families were relocated.

The site has been capped, and a drainage system has been installed to remove the toxic wastes as they leak out. The EPA's Superfund spent about $275 million of taxpayers' money to clean up the site. In 1990, the EPA declared part of the site habitable, and the area has been renamed Black Creek Village.

You can do many things to help reduce and dispose of hazardous wastes. Try some of the following ideas and activities on your own or with friends and classmates. Some of these activities mention organizations to write to, or you can contact some of the organizations in Appendix A for more information.

Things you can do

Read the instructions and warning labels of hazardous household products, such as cleaning fluids, paints, varnishes, and pesticides, before you buy or use them. Don't assume them to be safe. Be aware of the dangers to you while you are using a product and to the environment when it is disposed of.

Living green

Never pour hazardous chemicals, such as leftover cleaning fluids, paints, solvents, petroleum products, or pesticides, into the sink, toilet, or down a storm drain. Store these substances safely and take them to a proper hazardous waste facility for disposal.

Living green

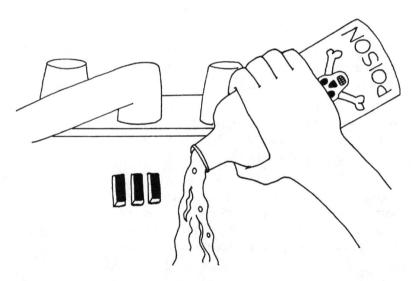

Don't pour hazardous liquids like cleaning fluids down a drain.

Participate in your local hazardous waste cleanup day or use special hazardous waste facilities in your area. If your community has no cleanup day or special facility, contact your town hall or environmental protection department and ask them for instructions. If local authorities cannot help, contact your state university's Cooperative Extension Service.

Activity

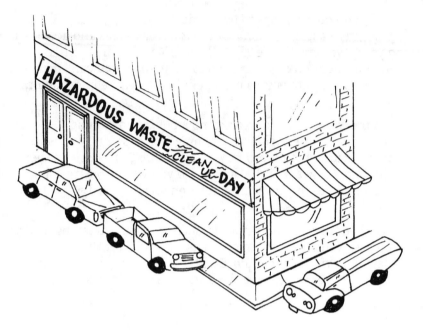

Participate in your town's hazardous waste cleanup day. If they don't have one, try to help organize one.

Activity   Become active in educating citizens about the hazardous waste disposal problem and help start new programs to reduce and properly dispose of hazardous wastes in your community.

Living green   Buy only the amount of hazardous substances, such as cleaning solutions and varnishes, that you will use. Few leftovers means less waste.

Living green   Use safe alternatives to hazardous chemicals whenever possible. Many cleaning fluids contain toxic chemicals. You can make or buy many nontoxic cleaning solutions. They do a good job without polluting our planet when they are discarded.

You can make a good all-around cleaning fluid for general home cleaning by mixing 1 gallon of hot water, ¼ cup of ammonia in which you have squirted a small amount of dishwashing liquid, ¼ cup of vinegar, and 1 tablespoon of baking soda.

Other safe cleaning solutions are listed here:

- For a furniture and floor polish, consider one of the commercial products available that uses lemon oil and beeswax in a mineral base.
- Vinegar works well as a toilet bowl cleaner.
- For glass cleaner, mix 2 tablespoons of borax in 3 cups of water and spray with a spray pump.

¼ cup ammonia   ¼ cup vinegar   1 tablespoon baking soda

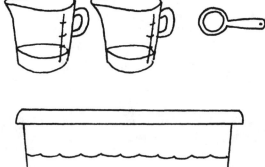

1 gallon hot water

Common household items can make a good general cleaning solution for your house.

Keep your sink drains clean in an environmentally safe way. Once a week, mix 1 cup of baking soda, 1 cup of salt, and ¼ cup of cream of tartar. Pour ¼ cup of this solution down each drain and follow with a pot of boiling water. If a drain ever does clog, use a plumber's snake instead of dangerous chemical cleaners,

Living green

which are usually still dangerous when they enter the environment as waste.

Living green   Instead of purchasing air fresheners, try fragrant candles or simmering potpourri ingredients, such as cinnamon, cloves, and orange peel. You can absorb bad smells in enclosed areas with an open box of baking soda.

Living green   Prevent leaking underground storage tanks. If you have an underground oil tank, ask your parents to check it for leaks. Be sure your local gasoline dealers are required to do the same for their gas tanks. Leaking underground storage tanks play a major role in contaminating our waters. For information about leaking tanks, contact the national bulletin at the New England Interstate Water Pollution Control Commission, 85 Merrimac Street, Boston, Massachusetts 02114.

Living green   Don't dump hazardous wastes directly on the ground. They will either seep down and contaminate groundwater or run off into a stream or river and kill aquatic life. Bring these substances to a recycling facility or a special hazardous waste collection facility. Contact your local government to see where the closest facility is located.

Bare facts   For decades, hazardous waste was disposed of by simply dumping it. Most of this waste was dumped into or onto the soil or stored in steel drums, which sooner or later corrode and leak. It is believed that about 2 percent of our groundwater is already contaminated with these wastes.

Hazardous wastes that are not dumped on or in the soil go directly into water. Much of it is simply released into rivers, streams, or even sewage systems, where it makes its way to the open waters. This waste damages or destroys many aquatic ecosystems. New methods of hazardous waste disposal are being tested and used in pilot programs. Many environmentalists feel the best solution for hazardous wastes is to use less of them in the first place.

Don't purchase smoke detectors that contain radioactive material. Most contain the radioactive element americium. When buying a new smoke detector, buy an *ionization detector*, which contains no hazardous radioactive material. No radioactive waste means no chance of contaminating the environment.

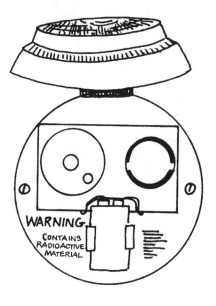

Most smoke detectors use a radioactive material (americium). Next time your family is looking to buy a smoke detector, consider one that does not use this material.

Educate yourself about home batteries. Reduce the use of batteries whenever possible. Americans buy 2 billion batteries each year. Most batteries contain mercury, which is toxic to all life. When the batteries are thrown away, the mercury enters the waste stream and makes its way into bodies of water. Use rechargeable batteries when possible. Even though they contain cadmium, which is also toxic, you'll need fewer batteries. Use solar cells when possible. Solar cells are often found in calculators and some other devices. These devices convert sunlight directly into electricity.

Purchase detergents that do not contain phosphates. Many powdered laundry soaps contain phosphates to soften the water. When phosphorus from these detergents goes down the drain, it passes through most sewage treatment plants and into a body of water. Phosphorus is a nutrient usually found in

Most household batteries contain mercury. Rechargeable batteries contain cadmium.

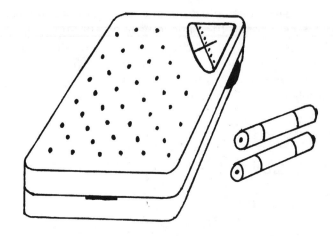

Some products, such as calculators, often come with solar cells and don't need any batteries.

BURST
CLOTHES DETERGENT
CONTAINS NO PHOSPHATES

Many detergents now contain no phosphates.

limited amounts in aquatic ecosystems. When phosphates in detergents are added to an ecosystem, there can be a population explosion of certain organisms that cause a chain reaction of events resulting in a lack of dissolved oxygen. This process can cause the death of a pond, lake, or even a portion of the coast. Look at the label for phosphate-free brands before buying.

Suggest that your class write letters to local officials to support the improvement of your town's sewage treatment plant by installing new tertiary treatment equipment. This equipment removes phosphates and other harmful substances from the treated water before it is released back into the environment.

Activity

Many states have passed laws that ban the use of phosphates in detergents and other products. Find out if your state has such laws. If not, have your class write to your elected state officials asking them to pass laws in your state.

Activity

Buy unbleached paper products. Paper is made pure white by a bleaching process that produces hazardous wastes. Dioxin is a very toxic chemical, created during the bleaching process. Unbleached paper products work just fine—they simply don't look pure white. Buy unbleached products like coffee filters, milk cartons, toilet paper, and paper towels. If more people used unbleached paper products, less bleaching would be needed, resulting in less hazardous waste.

Living green

 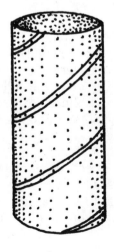

Bleaching paper produces deadly substances that make their way into our environment. Unbleached paper might not look as pretty, but making it does not harm the environment as much.

Hazardous wastes: Polluting our planet   97

Activity Have your class write to your elected officials asking them to support the continuation and strengthening of the Clean Water Act. This act restores and maintains clear, clean water. It protects our water by setting and enforcing standards for water quality.

Living green Make sure people dispose of used car oil properly. It is estimated that 50 percent of all car owners change their own oil. Most of this oil is improperly discarded by being placed into landfills, dumped into sewers, or simply dumped on the soil. If the 4 quarts of oil from one car were spilled in a lake, it would create an oil slick 8 acres in size! Used oil often finds its way into the nearest stream, where it can smother fish and other wildlife. Bottom dwellers such as oysters and clams are smothered as it settles on them.

Oil stunts the growth of or kills marsh grasses, which are important to aquatic ecosystems. Oil also releases toxic chemicals which can cause cancer in marine organisms. Many service stations have oil collection centers. For information, contact your local environmental protection department.

Bare facts Used oil can be recycled into new oil. It takes 42 gallons of new crude oil but only 2 gallons of used oil, to produce two quarts of fresh car oil. It also takes half as much energy to produce a quart of fresh oil from recycled oil than from virgin crude.

Science project: Oil slicks
Project overview When most people think about oil spills, they think about huge oil tankers like the Exxon *Valdez* spilling its load of oil into a harbor or the open sea. Far more oil and oil products make their way into bodies of water every year by less dramatic causes, such as boats flushing out their hulls or two-cycle engines, which mix oil and gasoline. These so-called normal releases of oil cause more environmental damage than any single oil spill from a tanker.

Water has a physical property called *surface tension*, which is caused by water molecules sticking together. Surface tension tends to make things "stick" to the water's surface like a leaf floating down a stream. Small organisms usually cannot escape

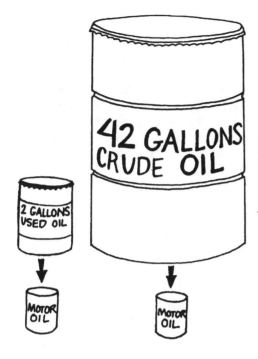

It takes 42 gallons of new oil, but only 2 gallons of used motor oil, to create 2 quarts of fresh motor oil.

this tension and become trapped in water. Some insects, however, depend on the surface tension of water to survive. Water striders, whirligig beetles, and springtails are examples of insects that live on top of the water and use surface tension to help them travel over the water.

Contaminants in water, such as oil or soap, reduce surface tension. What happens to aquatic insects that normally travel on top of water when the natural surface tension is destroyed by oil slick pollution? Can they still walk on water? What is your hypothesis?

Materials list

- Six live insects that live on the water's surface (collect these insects, such as water striders or whirligig beetles, or order them from a biological supply house). Catch them in a net because many can bite.
- Two containers that have the same surface area (use milk cartons cut in half).
- Measuring cup.

- Water.
- Vegetable oil.
- Liquid dish detergent.

Procedures If you need to cut milk cartons in half, ask an adult to help you. Put two cups of water in each container. Add three insects to each container. Spend at least 10 minutes observing the natural movements of the insects across the water. Carefully observe how the insect contacts the water. Note your observations in your project notebook.

After you have observed the insects, add a few squirts of liquid dish detergent to one container and a few tablespoons of oil to the other. Continue to add enough of each "pollutant" so the surface is covered. A thin film covering the entire surface is all you need. Observe the insects in each container. How is their movement and behavior different than before? Once again observe how the insects contact the water. Note your observations. Release the insects outside on a body of water when you are done.

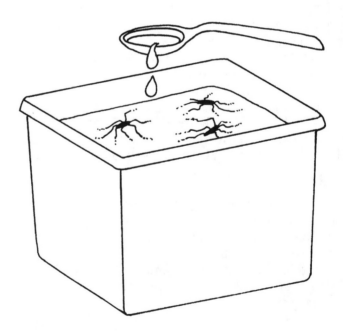

Add a few tablespoons of vegetable oil to the water's surface.

How did the insects move in or on the unpolluted water? How did they move after the pollutant spills? How does the movement differ? Could the water strider stride or the whirligig beetle whirl? Did one pollutant have more of an effect than the other? Research what happened to the surface tension and what effect it had on the insects. Was your hypothesis correct?

Conclusions

Save electricity: Fight acid rain & global warming

OUR SOCIETY runs on fossil fuels: coal, oil, and natural gas. We use coal and oil to generate electricity, oil and gas to heat our homes, and gasoline (from oil) to run our cars. But burning fossil fuels produces pollutants that cause acid rain and add carbon dioxide to the air, possibly causing global warming. One of the best ways to fight these types of environmental damages is to conserve electricity and look for other types of fuel to replace fossil fuels.

Fossil fuels include coal, oil, and natural gas.

acid rain When fossil fuels are burned in electric power plants and gasoline is burned in automobiles, pollutants are released into the air. These pollutants combine with each other to form other pollutants, including acids. When these acids combine with moisture in the air and fall as precipitation, the result is called *acid rain*.

Terms to know

Acid rain damages statues, but it also causes much more serious harm to our environment.

Rain that has the same acidity as grapefruit juice often falls in portions of the United States; weather stations on mountain tops in New Hampshire have recorded rain the acidity of lemon juice. Acid rain changes the acidity of ponds, lakes, and reservoirs. These changes kill fish and damage aquatic ecosystems. It is estimated that about 25,000 lakes in North America have been affected by acid rain. Reducing the demand for electricity reduces air pollutants that cause the acids. Conserving electricity helps protect aquatic ecosystems from acid rain.

global warming Certain gases in our planet's atmosphere trap heat, which maintains a relatively constant temperature. Since these gases act like a greenhouse, they are called *greenhouse gases* and trapping of heat is called the *greenhouse effect*.

Environmentalists know that burning fossil fuels over the past few hundred years has increased the amount of carbon dioxide (a greenhouse gas) in the atmosphere. Increased amounts of carbon dioxide and other greenhouse gases are likely to result in a gradual increase in the earth's surface temperature, a process called *global warming*.

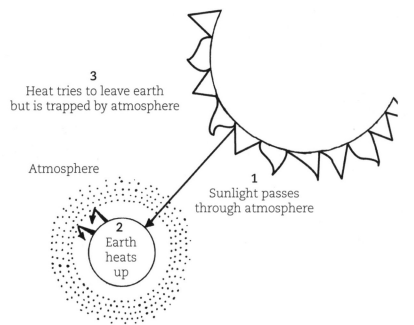

3
Heat tries to leave earth
but is trapped by atmosphere

Atmosphere

1
Sunlight passes
through atmosphere

2
Earth
heats
up

The greenhouse effect traps heat in our atmosphere much like a greenhouse traps heat.

Still other causes of global warming are changing natural cycles. Deforestation is believed to account for about 20 percent of the global warming. Plants take in carbon dioxide during photosynthesis. Fewer trees means less intake of carbon dioxide.

Very small changes to the earth's surface temperature can have dramatic effects, such as melting of the ice caps and a rising sea level. Global warming would change the face of our planet and the way people and all animals live on it.

You can do many things to help save electricity. Try some of the following ideas and activities on your own or with friends and classmates. Some of these activities mention organizations to write to, or you can contact some of the organizations in Appendix A for more information.

Things you can do

Replace old light bulbs with compact fluorescent bulbs or the new E-lamp (radio wave) bulbs to conserve electricity and reduce pollutants that cause acid rain. Even though these bulbs

Living green

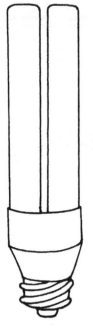

The compact fluorescent bulb is much more economical than the standard type of light bulb over time.

are more expensive, they last much longer and are far cheaper in the long run.

Living green   In cold climates, save electricity by preventing heat loss. Use insulation, caulking, and weatherstripping materials. Use energy-efficient air-conditioning units in hot climates.

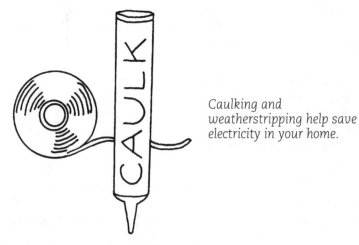

Caulking and weatherstripping help save electricity in your home.

Save hot water by using less of it and insulating more. Research passive and active hot water heating systems. See if anyone in your class has alternative types of hot water systems designed to conserve electricity.

Living green

Suggest to your parents that your family use cars less. Try riding a bike more often. Locate and use paths and trails designated for bike travel. Contact the Rails-to-Trails Conservancy, 1400 16th Street, NW, Suite 300, Washington, D.C. 20036.

Living green

One of the best ways to pollute less is to get more people to ride bikes instead of driving cars.

Investigate battery-powered automobiles. When are they going to become available to the public? Contact auto manufacturers for details. How will battery-powered cars compare in performance and in price to the conventional gasoline-powered car? Ask your classmates to ask their parents if they would buy an electric car in the near future. How many would and how many would not? Why or why not?

Activity

Check your refrigerator for leaks. Hold a dollar bill halfway in and halfway out of the refrigerator and close the door. If you can easily slide the bill out of the door, the seals should be replaced. Cleaning the coils will make the refrigerator run more efficiently as well.

Living green

Go to appliance stores and read the energy labels on new appliances. Study and compare the costs of the most efficient with the least efficient. If you had to pay more for an energy-efficient appliance, how long would it take for you to make up the difference by saving on electricity bills? How much

Activity

The dollar bill test is a simple way to see if your refrigerator is sealed properly.

Most large appliances have energy efficiency labels.

electricity would your entire class save if everyone changed over to energy-efficient refrigerators?

Bare facts Wind energy power plants in California consist of 16,000 wind turbines covering acres of desert land. These modern-day windmills generate enough power to provide electricity to a city the size of San Francisco.

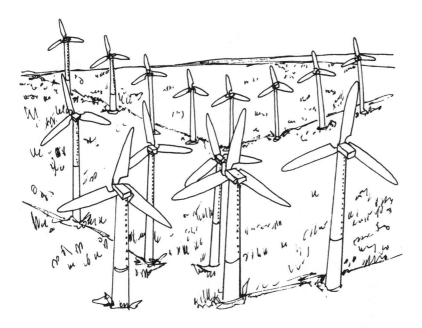

A wind power farm in southern California has 16,000 wind turbines.

Suggest that your class write to your elected officials asking them to support legislation to fund research and development of solar and wind power and to tax the excessive use of fossil fuels.

Activity

Investigate advances in solar cell technology (photovoltaic cells) like those found in many pocket calculators. Do they show any promise in replacing fossil fuels or can they only calculate numbers?

Living green

Research other energy alternatives called *cool energy*, which do not contribute to global warming. What does the *cool* refer to? For information about cool energy contact the Union of Concerned Scientists, 26 Church Street, Cambridge, Massachusetts 02238.

Living green

About 80 percent of our energy needs come from fossil fuels. Fossil fuels include coal, oil, and natural gas. The use of fossil fuels in automobiles and in electric power plants are the primary cause of air pollution today. Cars and electric power

Science fair project: Solar energy
Project overview

plants produce many of pollutants responsible for air pollution, acid rain, and global warming.

To reduce our need for fossil fuels, new types of power are being researched and developed. They include solar, hydroelectric (water), geothermal, wind, and biomass (plant material and animal waste) power. Some people believe that environmentally clean solar power will be the answer to all our energy needs in the future.

One way of using solar energy is to use solar cells—the kind you might find on a pocket calculator. But can you use a solar cell to light a small light bulb? If so, how can you position the solar cell to generate the most power? What are your hypotheses?

Materials list
- A solar cell (can be purchased at electronics stores, hobby shops, auto parts stores, or boat dealers).
- Lamp bulb. (It must have a compatible voltage rating with the solar cell. Buy them together to ensure that they match. You'll probably need to use a small flashlight bulb.)
- Lamp socket to hold the light bulb.
- Multimeter (to read voltage) or voltage meter available in your school.
- Electrical wiring.
- A wooden board large enough to mount the solar cell, lamp socket, and multimeter.
- A few screws or nails for mounting.
- An outdoor table.
- A protractor to measure angles.

Procedures
Get an adult to help you set up the apparatus. Attach the solar panel, lamp socket, and multimeter to the board as seen on page 111. Once they are all attached to the board, wire the three devices together as seen in the illustration. (The wiring must be done with the help of a knowledgeable adult.)

Once the apparatus is put together, take it outdoors around noon on a clear, sunny day. Place the device on a table and angle the board so the solar cell is aimed directly toward the

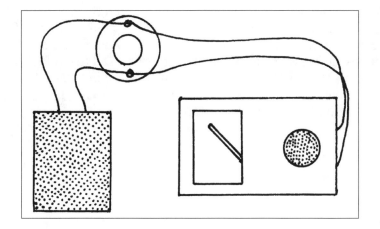

Mount the solar cell, bulb socket, and multimeter onto the board.

sun. Does the bulb light up? Record your answer, and then read the voltage reading on the multimeter. Use a protractor to measure the angle between the board and the table. This angle is the sun's "altitude." Write all this information down in your notebook.

Next, determine how the cell's angle to the sun affects the amount of energy generated by the solar cell. Be sure the panel is facing the sun. Use the protractor to move the angle of the apparatus board at intervals of 10 degrees.

For each observation, measure the voltage on the multimeter, the angle between the board and the table, and the brightness of the bulb.

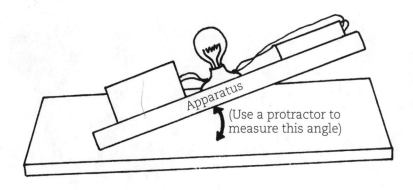

Apparatus
(Use a protractor to measure this angle)

Angle the apparatus board upward 10 degrees toward the sun. See if the bulb is lit and read the voltage on the meter.

Conclusions   Did the bulb light up with the solar panel directly facing the sun? How much voltage was generated? How did the angle of the solar cell to the sun affect the voltage? Was there a big difference between each 10-degree interval? Did the bulb light up at all angles? How important is the positioning of solar cells in creating electricity? Was your hypothesis correct?

Conserving water: Our most valuable resource

EACH PERSON in the United States uses roughly 65 gallons of water each and every day. Not long ago, most people thought that the earth had an endless supply of water. Today, in many parts of the United States and throughout the world, water is in short supply and is being used far more quickly than nature can replace it.

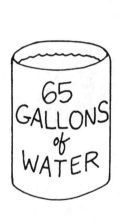

Every man, woman, and child in the United States uses about 65 gallons of water each and every day of the year.

Many parts of the United States do not have enough drinking water. Cities remove millions of gallons of water from rivers and even change the direction of rivers. Some of these rivers never even make it to the ocean. Water shortages are a way of life in some parts of the country and will get worse as our population continues to grow.

Using a lot of water not only means water shortages but also more wastewater. Wastewater is usually treated in sewage treatment plants and then returned to our environment (streams, rivers, and coastal waters). This treated water still pollutes our environment.

Terms to know   **groundwater and surface water**   Fresh water on our planet is divided into two groups: surface water and groundwater. *Surface water* includes streams, rivers, ponds, lakes, reservoirs, and oceans. *Groundwater* refers to water that seeps into the earth and is stored in natural underground reservoirs called *aquifers*. Both types of water are used equally for drinking water supplies.

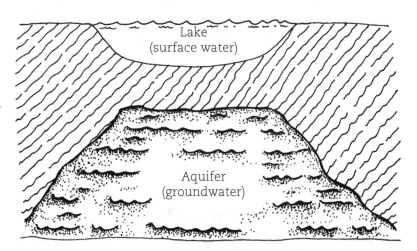

In the United States, we get about 50 percent of our drinking water from surface waters (lakes, reservoirs) and the other 50 percent from groundwater.

Pesticides, chemicals from industry (dioxin, for example), and heavy metals (such as mercury from batteries) pollute both types of water. Surface water is polluted when chemicals are carried with rainwater into streams and rivers. If these chemicals soak into the ground, they can pollute the groundwater.

aquifer   Almost all of the U.S. freshwater supply and about half of the drinking water comes from groundwater. Large areas of groundwater are called *aquifers*. Aquifers are not actual bodies of water, as many people think, but instead are large areas of permeable rock, gravel, or sand that are soaked with water,

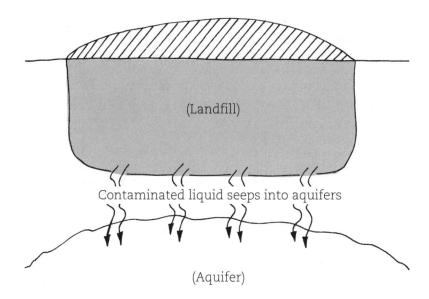

(Landfill)

Contaminated liquid seeps into aquifers

(Aquifer)

Landfills often leak pollutants into the earth, where they make their way into the groundwater.

much like a wet sponge. Aquifers can cover only a few square miles or thousands of square miles. The Ogallala aquifer reaches from South Dakota to Texas.

Both the quantity and quality of groundwater in aquifers has been changed by humans. The amount of groundwater removed in the United States jumped from 30 billion to more than 70 billion gallons per day between 1950 and 1985. In most areas, more groundwater is being extracted than nature can replace.

Pesticides, fertilizers, leaking septic tanks, and toxic waste from landfills are contaminating aquifers across the country. Other causes of contaminated aquifers are the numerous abandoned hazardous waste disposal sites around the country and the practice of injecting toxic wastes into deep underground wells.

You can do many things to help conserve water. Try some of the following ideas and activities on your own or with friends and classmates. Some of these activities mention organizations to write to, or you can contact some of the organizations in Appendix A for more information.

Things you can do

Living green　Conserve water whenever you take a shower by replacing old shower heads with low-flow heads. A five-minute shower with most older shower heads uses about 25 gallons of water. New low-flow shower heads save about 26,000 gallons of water a year for a family of four. Besides saving water and reducing pollution, low-flow shower heads will save your family money on water bills.

Some homes are not hooked up to the town's sewer system. They have a septic tank that captures solids and a septic field that distributes wastewater underground. If you have a septic field, a low-flow shower head will increase the life of your system. A list of low-flow shower head vendors is available from the National Wildlife Federation, 1400 16th Street, NW, Washington, D.C. 20036.

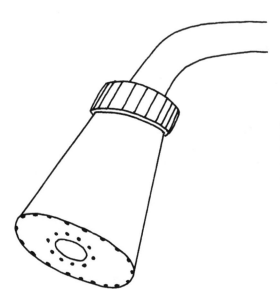

New low-flow shower heads reduce the amount of water used, but they still work well.

Living green　Conserve water in your home's toilet. A typical toilet uses 5 gallons per flush. You can easily save about 20 percent of this water by placing a plastic bottle filled with water (and a few rocks for stability) in the tank to reduce the volume of water. A family of four could save 7,000 gallons of water each year by placing a bottle in the tank.

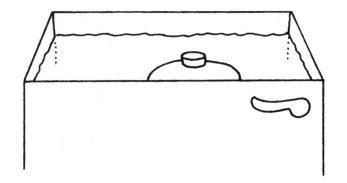

A plastic bottle filled with water and a few stones will reduce the amount of water used during each flush.

For new construction, install low-flush toilets, which save 75 percent of the 40,000 gallons of water a family of four flushes down the toilet each year. They use less than 2 gallons of water with each flush.

Activity

Figure out how much water would be saved if everyone in your class was to lower the amount of water used while flushing the toilet bowl in their homes. How much water would be saved if everyone in your school or even everyone in your town or city was to do this? Do you think it would make a big difference?

Activity

See if your toilet bowl is leaking by putting a few drops of food color in the tank behind the bowl. Wait a few minutes to see if any of the dye has made its way into the bowl. If so, the toilet has a leak that should be repaired to conserve water.

Living green

Don't leave the water running when you brush your teeth. If you must wait for the water to get hot to wash your hands or face, brush your teeth while you are waiting. Have family members who shave conserve water as well by not letting water run.

Living green

If you have a dishwasher, use it instead of washing the dishes by hand. A dishwasher usually uses less water than hand washing. Only run the dishwasher when it is fully loaded.

Place a few drops of food coloring in the tank of the toilet. Wait a few minutes to see if the color leaks into the bowl.

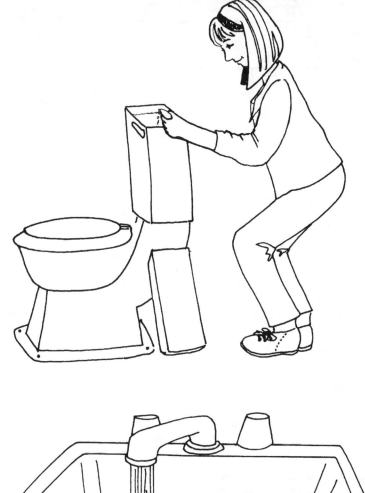

Don't leave the water running while you are brushing your teeth, or you will needlessly waste water.

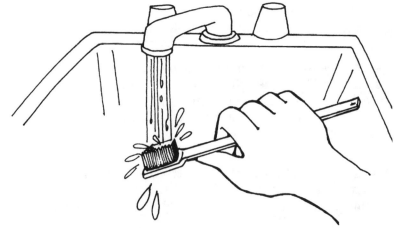

If you wash dishes by hand, don't leave the water running. Help conserve water. Fill the sink with soapy water and rinse separately.

When using a dishwasher, use shorter cycles. Don't use the rinse hold cycle—it wastes water. When your family is purchasing a new dishwasher, look for water-conserving features. Newer washers have many options to save water.

If you know someone who is purchasing a clothes washing machine, suggest that they buy a front loader. Front loaders usually use far less water than top-loading machines. When you and your family do laundry, wash only full loads and use all the water-conserving features that are available on your machine.

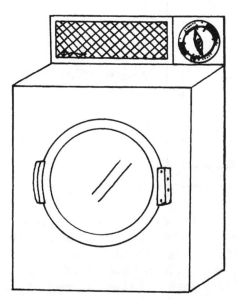

Front-loading washers use much less water than top loaders.

Repair leaky faucets right away. A dripping faucet can waste 20 gallons of water a day. Check outdoor faucets as well as those in the home. Search for other leaks by looking for leaking shower heads or leaks at the seams of pipes in your basement.

Living green   Install a flow control aerator on all faucets to reduce the flow of water. About 4 gallons of water pass through the typical faucet per minute. The flow on a faucet with an aerator is reduced to about ½ to 1 gallon per minute.

Living green   If you must let water run to get cold water to drink, fill a bottle with water and leave it in the refrigerator. It will taste more refreshing and conserve water as well.

Living green   Encourage water metering in your area. Studies show that homes with meters use 55 percent less water than unmetered homes. Suggest to your town officials that the water supply be metered.

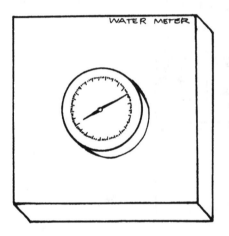

Water meters conserve water use.

Living green   Avoid using a garbage disposal whenever possible. They waste excessive amounts of water. The wastewater produced is rich in nutrients (from leftover food) that are difficult to remove in sewage treatment plants. These additional nutrients damage aquatic ecosystems. Consider setting up a compost heap for your leftover food scraps.

Living green   Make sure your home's septic tank is properly maintained. The septic tank should be pumped out routinely. Septic systems allow the wastewater from your home to be slowly released into the soil. As this wastewater filters through the soil, it is attacked by bacteria that break down the organic matter, making the water safe for the environment.

Maintaining your home's septic system can save your family thousands of dollars and help protect the environment at the same time. Overflowing septic systems release nutrients into the water that run off into streams and rivers.

To keep a septic system working efficiently, your family should follow these guidelines:

- Don't use a garbage disposal.
- Don't flush sanitary napkins, tampons, cigarettes, or disposable diapers down the toilet.
- Don't dump grease or oils of any kind in the sink or toilet.
- Don't put disinfectants, pesticides, medicines, or paint thinners down the drain because they kill the microbes that break down sewage.
- Keep deep-rooted trees away from the drainage system.
- Don't allow heavy vehicles to travel over the drainage fields.

Activity

Have your class write letters to your elected officials asking them to support new laws that reduce the use of water by farms and industry. The largest use of water is irrigation for farms; next comes industry. These businesses should conserve water whenever possible.

Living green

Check with a lawn-care specialist to see how much water is needed for your home's grass and shrubs. Most people overwater, in many cases doing more harm than good. The United States has 10 million acres of lawn. During the hot summer months, many people water their lawns using more water than all other forms of residential water use combined. We can save vast amounts of water by watering lawns and shrubs only when necessary.

Activity

Survey your classmates to find out how often their family waters the lawn in the summer. Then check with a specialist to see how much they should water their lawns. Determine how much water is wasted and how much can be conserved by your classmates alone. Then figure out how much can be saved by your entire school or town, if everyone began watering their lawns with the correct amount of water.

Living green Plant with water conservation in mind. When planting grasses or shrubs, think about their watering requirements. Some do very well with little water. For example, red fescue grass, English ivy, periwinkle ground cover, and euonymous shrubs do fine during dry spells. Some types of grasses stop growing in droughts but revive when the water returns. Ask your local lawn-care specialist about the best types of grasses and shrubs for your area.

Science project: Dripping water
Project overview Water shortages are an important environmental problem in many parts of our country and the world. Everyone should be concerned about water conservation. We've all seen dripping faucets in sinks, shower heads, and tubs. Are these tiny little drips a serious problem? How much water does a single dripping faucet lose? How much would a single dripping faucet in each of your classmates' homes lose in one week, one month, and one year? What about a single leak in each home in your town over a year's time? What are your hypotheses?

Materials list
- Faucet
- Pots or bowls
- Calculator
- Graduated cylinder or other measuring cup
- Stopwatch or a watch with a second hand
- A library to do some fact finding

Procedures With your parents' permission, use a faucet in your home to create a drip. (If you already have a dripping faucet in your home or school, see if you can use it.) Turn the water on to make the water drip consistently as if it had a very slow leak. Once the water appears to be in a slow but steady drip, you can continue.

Place an empty pot or bowl beneath the leak and immediately begin timing three minutes. After three minutes remove the pot. (Leave the water dripping, though.) Use the graduated cylinder to measure the amount of water that leaked out of the faucet during the three-minute test period. Repeat this procedure at least five times to get the average amount of water for three minutes. Next, divide the amount of water lost in three minutes by three to find out how much water was lost per minute by this leak.

Once you have this number, you can do some more math. How much water is lost each day from this one dripping faucet? How about each week, month, and year? What if every classmate had one leaking faucet in their home? Multiply the yearly amount by the number of your classmates. How much water is lost if every home in your town or city had one leaking faucet? Go to your library to find out the number of homes in your town. How much water would be lost each year in your town?

Are small drips a serious water conservation problem? Was your hypothesis correct? Ask your classmates to look in their homes for leaky faucets. How many are actually found? Is one leaky faucet per home a good estimate? Read more about water shortages and water conservation in the home.

Conclusions

Organizations
to contact

See various entries throughout the book for more organizations to contact.

American Association of Zoological Parks & Aquariums
Oglebay Park
Wheeling, WV 26003

*Protecting
marine life*

American Cetacean Society
Box 2639
San Pedro, CA 90731

Animal Protection Institute of America
P.O. Box 22505
Sacramento, CA 95822

Animal Welfare Institute
P.O. Box 3650
Washington, DC 20007

California Academy of Sciences
Golden Gate Park
San Francisco, CA 94118

California Center for Wildlife
76 Albert Park Ln.
P.O. Box 957
San Rafael, CA 94915

Center for Action on Endangered Species
175 W. Main St., NW
Ayer, MA 01432

Center for Coastal Studies
Cetacean Research Program
59 Commercial St., Box 826
Provincetown, MA 02657

Center for Marine Conservation
Atlantic Coast Office
1725 DeSales St., NW
Suite 500
Washington, DC 20036

Center for Marine Conservation
Pacific Coast Office
580 Market St., Suite 550
San Francisco, CA 94104

Cetacean Society International
P.O. Box 953
Georgetown, CT 06829

Defenders of Wildlife
1244 19th St., NW
Washington, DC 20036

Earth Island Institute
International Marine Mammal Project
300 Broadway, Suite 28
San Francisco, CA 94133

The Entanglement Network
c/o Defenders of Wildlife
1244 19th St., NW
Washington, DC 20036
(202) 659-9510

Environmental Defense Fund
1616 P St., NW
Washington, DC 20006

Friends of the Sea Otter
P.O. Box 221220
Carmel, CA 93922

Greenpeace U.S.A.
1611 Connecticut Ave., NW
Washington, DC 20009

Humane Society of the U.S.
2100 L St., NW
Washington, DC 20037

International Fund for Animal Welfare
P.O. Box 193
Yarmouth Port, MA 02675

International Wildlife Coalition
Whale Adoption Project
634 North Falmouth Hwy.
P.O. Box 388
North Falmouth, MA 02556-0388

Marine Mammal Center
Marin Headlands
Golden Gate National Recreation Area
Sausalito, CA 94965

Marine Mammal Fund
Fort Mason Center, Bldg. E
San Francisco, CA 94123

Marine World—Africa U.S.A.
1000 Fairgrounds
Vallejo, CA 94589

Monterey Bay Aquarium
886 Cannery Row
Monterey, CA 93940

National Wildlife Federation
1412 16th St., NW
Washington, DC 20036

The Oceanic Society
1536 16th St., NW
Washington, DC 20036

Pacific Whale Foundation
Kealia Beach Plaza, Suite 21
101 Noth Kihei Rd.
Kihei, Maui, HI 96753

Point Reyes Bird Observatory
4990 Shoreline Hwy.
Sinson Beach, CA 94970

Save the Manatee Club
500 N. Maitland Ave.
Maitland, FL 32751

Save the Whale, Inc.
P.O. Box 2397
Venice, CA 90291

Sea Shepherd Conservation Society
1314 Second St.
Santa Monica, CA 90401

Sea Turtle Center
P.O. Box 634
Nevada City, CA 95959

Suncoast Seabird Sanctuary
18328 Gulf Blvd.
Indian Shores, FL 34635

Stripers Unlimited
880 Washington St.
P.O. Box 3045
South Attleboro, MA 02703

Tarlton Foundation
1160 Battery St., Suite 360
San Francisco, CA 94111

Trout Unlimited
800 Follin Ln., Suite 250
Vienna, VA 22180

Wildlife Conservation International
New York Zoological Society
Bronx Zoo
Bronx, NY 10460

American Groundwater Trust
6375 Riverside Dr.
Dublin, OH 43017

American Water Resources Association
5410 Grosvenor Ln., Suite 220
Bethesda, MD 20814

Center for the Great Lakes
435 N. Michigan Ave., Suite 1408
Chicago, IL 60611

Chesapeake Bay Foundation
162 Prince George St.
Annapolis, MD 21401

Chesapeake Bay Trust
60 West St., Suite 200-A
Annapolis, MD 21401

Clean Water Action, Inc.
317 Pennsylvania Ave., SE
Washington, DC 20003

Clean Water Act Network
1350 New York Ave., NW, Suite #300
Washington, DC 20005

Freshwater Foundation
725 Country Rd., Six
Wayzta, MN 55391

Friends of the River
Fort Mason Center, Bldg. C
San Francisco, CA 94123

Protecting water quality

Great Lakes United
Buffalo State College
Cassety Hall
1300 Elmwood Ave.
Buffalo, NY 14222

Long Island Sound Taskforce
Oceanic Society
185 Magee Ave.
Stamford Marine Center
Stamford, CT 06902

North American Lake Management Society
One Progress Blvd., Box 27
Alachua, FL 32615

Puget Sound Alliance
130 Nickerson, Suite 107
Seattle, WA 98109

Ocean Ark International
One Locust St.
Falmouth, MA 02540

Protecting Bodies of Water
American Rivers
801 Pennsylvania Ave., SE
Suite 400
Washington, DC 20003

River Network
P.O. Box 8787
Portland, OR 97207

Education & research

American Fisheries Society
5410 Grosvenor Ln.
Bethesda, MD 20814

American Littoral Society
Sandy Hook
Highlands, NJ 07732

California Coastal Commission
45 Fremont St.
Suite 2000
San Francisco, CA 95105

Center for Coastal Studies
59 Commerce St.
Box 1036
Provincetown, MA 02657

Coast Alliance
235 Pennsylvania Ave., SE
Washington, DC 20003

Coastal Resource Center
P.O. Box 3084
San Rafael, CA 94912

Cousteau Society, Inc.
930 West 21st St.
Norfolk, VA 23517

National Coalition for Marine Conservation, Inc.
P.O. Box 23298
Savannah, GA 31403

National Oceanographic and Atmospheric Administration
(NOAA)
Herbert Hoover Bldg., Room 5128
14th and Constitution Ave., NW
Washington, DC 20230

Woods Hole Oceanographic Institution
Woods Hole, MA 02543

Center for Plastics Recycling Research   **Plastics &**
Building 3529 Busch Campus   **recycling**
Rutgers University
Piscataway, NJ 08855
(201) 932-4402

Coalition for Recyclable Waste
c/o Environmental Action Foundation
1525 New Hampshire Ave., NW
Washington, DC 20036
(202) 745-4879

Council on Plastics Packaging in the Environment
1275 K St., NW
Washington, DC 20005
(202) 371-5228

Environmental Action Foundation
1525 New Hampshire Ave.
Washington, DC 20036

INFORM, Inc.
381 Park Ave. S, Suite 1201
New York, NY 10016

Keep America Beautiful, Inc.
Mill River Plaza
9 W. Broad St.
Stamford, CT 06902

National Association for Plastic Container Recovery
P.O. Box 7784
Charlotte, NC 28241
(704) 523-8543

National Recycling Coalition
1101 30th St., NW
Washington, DC 20007

National Solid Waste Management Association
1730 Rhode Island Ave., NW
Washington, DC 20036

NOAA's Marine Debris Information Office
c/o Center for Marine Conservation
1725 DeSales St., NW
Washington, DC 20036

Society of the Plastics Industry
1275 K St., NW, #400
Washington, DC 20005
(202) 371-5200

Waste Management
1155 Connecticut Ave., #800
Washington, DC 20036

Citizen's Clearinghouse for Hazardous Wastes
P.O. Box 926
Arlington, VA 22216
(703) 276-7070

Hazardous wastes

Citizens for a Better Environment
33 E. Congress St.
Chicago, IL 60605

Clean Sites, Inc.
1199 North Fairfax
Alexandria, VA 22314

Hazardous Materials Control Research Institute
7237 Hanover Pkwy.
Greenbelt, MD 20770

Environmental Defense Fund
444 Park Ave., S.
New York, NY 10016

Environmental legislation

Natural Resources Defense Council
40 W. 20th St.,11th Fl.
New York, NY 10011
(212) 727-2700

National Coalition Against the Misuse of Pesticides
530 7th St., SE
Washington, DC 20003

Pesticides & toxic wastes

National Toxics Campaign
37 Temple Place, 4th Fl.
Boston, MA 02111

Northwest Coalition for Alternatives to Pesticides
P.O. Box 1393
Eugene, OR 97440

Pesticide Action Network
965 Mission St.
San Francisco, CA 94103

Scientific supply houses

You can order equipment, supplies, and live specimens for projects in this book from these companies.

Blue Spruce Biological Supply Co.
221 South St.
Castle Rock, CO 80104
(800) 621-8385

Carolina Biological Supply Co.
2700 York Rd.
Burlington, NC 27215
Eastern U.S.: 800-334-5551
Western U.S.: 800-547-1733

Connecticut Valley Biological
82 Valley Rd.
P.O. Box 326
Southampton, MA 01073

Fisher Scientific
4901 W. LeMoyne St.
Chicago, IL 60651
800-955-1177

Frey Scientific Co.
905 Hickory Ln.
P.O. Box 8101
Mansfield, OH 44901
(800) 225-FREY

Nasco
901 Janesville Ave.
P.O. Box 901
Fort Atkinson, WI 53538
(800) 558-9595

Nebraska Scientific
3823 Leavenworth St.
Omaha, NE 68105
(800) 228-7117

Powell Laboratories Division
19355 McLoughlin Blvd.
Gladstone, OR 97027
(800) 547-1733

Sargent-Welch Scientific Co.
P.O. Box 1026
Skokie, IL 60076

Southern Biological Supply Co.
P.O. Box 368
McKenzie, TN 38201
(800) 748-8735

Ward's Natural Science Establishment, Inc.
5100 West Henrietta Rd.
Rochester, NY 14692
(800) 962-2660

or

815 Fiero Ln.
P.O. Box 5010
San Luis Obispo, CA 93403
(800) 872-7289

Using metrics

Most science fairs require all measurements be taken using the metric system instead of English units. Meters and grams, which are based on powers of 10, are actually far easier to use during your experimentation than feet and pounds.

You can convert English units into metric units if need be, but it is easier to simply begin with metric units. If you are using school equipment, such as flasks or cylinders, check the markings to see if any use metric units. If you are purchasing your glassware (or plastic ware) be sure to order metric markings.

Conversions from English units to metric units are given below, along with their abbreviations as used in this book. (All conversions are approximations.)

one inch (in.) = 2.54 centimeters (cm)   **Length**
one foot (ft) = 30 cm
one yard (yd) = 0.90 meters (m)
one mile (mi) = 1.6 kilometers (km)

one teaspoon (tsp) = 5 milliliters (ml)   **Volume**
one tablespoon (tbsp or T) = 15 ml
one fluid ounce (fl. oz.) = 30 ml
one cup (C) = 0.24 liters (l)
one pint (pt) = 0.47 l
one quart (qt) = 0.95 l
one gallon (gal) = 3.80 l

one ounce (oz) = 28 grams (g)   **Mass**
one pound (lb) = 0.45 kilograms (kg)

32 degrees Fahrenheit (°F) = 0 degrees Celsius (°C)   **Temperature**
212 degrees F = 100 degrees C

abstract   A brief written overview that describes your project. An abstract is usually less than 250 words and is often required at science fairs.

acid rain   When fossil fuels (coal, oil, and natural gas) are burned, many pollutants are released into the air. These pollutants travel through the air and combine with each other, creating acids. When these acids fall to earth with rain, the result is called *acid rain*. Since these acids also come to the earth's surface in the form of snow, fog, dew, or small droplets, the phrase *acid deposition* is often used.

algae   Algae are primitive aquatic plants ranging from microscopic single-celled organisms to large multicelled plants, such as seaweed. Algae is of great importance in many aquatic ecosystems because it fills the role of the *producers* (green plants).

backboard   The vertical, self-supporting panel used in your science fair display. The board provides explanations that describe the project. It can include the problem studied, your hypothesis, photographs of the experimental setup, organisms used, analyzed data in the form of charts and tables, and other important aspects of the project. Most fairs have size limitations for this board.

bacteria   Bacteria are single-celled, microscopic organisms found in most environments in vast numbers. They reproduce by simply dividing (*fission*). Bacteria play an important role in food webs because they *decompose* (break down) dead plants and animals and return chemicals to the soil to be used by other plants.

bioaccumulation   Many pesticides remain toxic (poisonous) for long periods of time. These pesticides remain on plants, where they are eaten and absorbed into the animal's fatty tissue, where they remain. This gradual buildup of pesticides within an animal's body is called *bioaccumulation*. These accumulations can harm the animal or be passed on to a predator that eats the animal in a process called *biomagnification*.

biocontrol Also called *biological control*. Before chemicals became the standard method of controlling insect pests, people used natural methods. These natural methods have been advanced with science and technology and are now being used to control pests without chemicals. Biocontrol uses beneficial insects and other organisms to control pests.

biodegradable Refers to the ability of a substance or product to naturally break down (*decompose*) into basic elements or compounds so they can be reused as nutrients by plants. This breakdown occurs when bacteria and other microbes feed on the substance.

biodiversity Refers to the diversity of organisms on our planet and implies the importance of all.

biological categories Most science fairs categorize projects according to subject area. Awards are usually given in each subject area.

bioremediation The use of organisms to clean up waste products like oil spills or radioactive materials.

biosphere That portion of our planet that contains life.

bycatch Some methods of harvesting fish and shrimp result in capturing unwanted species. The unwanted organisms are called *bycatch*. The bycatch is thrown back into the water, usually dead or injured. Hundreds of millions of pounds of bycatch are wasted annually. Common bycatch include dolphins, marine turtles, and numerous species of fish and mammals.

Carson, Rachel A marine biologist and writer, Rachel Carson is best known for her 1962 book *Silent Spring*. In this book, she described how pesticides cause long-term hazards to birds, fish, other wildlife, and humans.

clear-cutting Clear-cutting is a logging method in which every tree in a region is cut. It is one of the oldest methods of harvesting forests and is used around the world. Clear-cutting is the least expensive way to remove wood. It is, however, devastating to the forest ecosystem. The habitat of most animals is destroyed, and the ecosystem for the entire region is affected. Clear-cutting results in soil erosion, making it impossible for the ecosystem to recover.

community   All the populations living within a specified area make up a community.

composting   The process of decomposing organic wastes such as leftover foods, grass clippings, leaves, and sewage sludge into a rich, fertile soil.

conservation tillage   Conventional tilling used on farms invites soil erosion since it involves turning over the soil in the fall, leaving it bare through the winter, and planting crops in the spring. Conservation tillage methods use special tillers that don't disturb the surface layer, leaving a protective layer of organic matter. Seeds, fertilizers, and pesticides are injected through the surface layer to the layer below. Leaving the top layer intact greatly reduces the amount of erosion.

consumer   Organisms can be categorized according to how they obtain energy to survive. *Consumers* are animals that must consume plants or other animals to obtain their energy. In contrast, *producers* capture energy from the sun during photosynthesis.

control group   A test group that offers a baseline for comparison, in which no experimental factors or stimulus are introduced.

dependent variable   A variable that changes when the experimental (independent) variable changes. For example, in the mortality (death) rate of organisms living in soil exposed to pesticides, the mortality rate is the dependent variable and the pesticides are the experimental variable.

detritus   Decomposing organic matter.

display   The entire science fair exhibit, of which the backboard is a part.

ecosystem The living (organisms) and nonliving (soil, water, etc.) components of a specified area, such as a pond or forest, and interactions that exist between all these components.

environmental literacy A basic level of understanding a person should have to make intelligent decisions about managing our environment.

experimental group A test group that is subjected to experimental factors or stimulus for the sake of comparison with the control group.

experimental variable Also called the *independent variable*. The aspect or factor to be changed for comparison.

fertilizer A substance added to the soil to supply nutrients required for plant growth. Fertilizers can be organic or synthetic.

food web A simple representation of "who eats what" in an ecosystem. Food chains show one-to-one associations, but food webs show multiple associations. In other words, a food web is all the food chains linked together.

fossil fuels Includes oil, coal, and natural gas. These fuels are all nonrenewable since their deposits are not being replenished.

fungus Primitive plants that cannot photosynthesize their own food. Most are *saprophytic*, meaning they feed on decaying plants and organic matter. They reproduce asexually with spores.

groundwater Water found beneath the earth's surface. Only one half of one percent of all water is groundwater, but it supplies 50 percent of all drinking water in the United States.

habitat Refers to the place an organism lives, for example, an aquatic or terrestrial habitat.

heavy metals These substances are natural elements such as lead, mercury, and nickel, which are mined from the earth and used in a vast array of products and manufacturing processes.

These substances enter organisms through the air, on food, in water, or by absorption directly through the skin.

hypothesis An educated guess formulated after thorough research, to be shown true or false through experimentation.

indigenous Organisms that naturally live in an area, as opposed to foreign or exotic species that are introduced from elsewhere.

indoor pollution A negative change in our indoor environment, where we spend 90 percent of our time. Indoor pollution is primarily caused by the excessive use of harmful substances in building and furniture materials and by poor ventilation.

inorganic matter Substances that are not alive and did not come from decomposed organisms.

journal The project notebook containing all notes on all aspects of a science fair project from start to finish.

leachate The contaminated liquid that accumulates at the bottom of a landfill, which often leaks into the groundwater supply.

leaf litter Partially decomposed leaves, twigs, and other plant matter that have recently fallen to the ground, forming a ground cover.

nitrogen-fixation Plants and animals need nitrogen to live, but the nitrogen in the air is in a form that cannot be used by living things. Some plants (along with bacteria that live in their roots) can change the nitrogen in the air into a form that can be used by living things. This process is called *nitrogen-fixation*.

organic Substances that compose living, dead, or decaying organisms and their waste products. Carbon is the primary element of an organic substance.

parasite An organism that lives in or on one or more organisms (host) for a portion of its life. The host is not killed in the process.

parasitoid An insect that lives in another organism (host) and kills its host during the parasitoid's development.

pathogens Organisms that cause disease in other organisms.

peat Rich soil composed of at least 50 percent organic matter.

population All members of the same species living within a specific area.

population dynamics The study of populations and factors that affect them.

pheromone A chemical that communicates information between members of the same species.

predator An animal that eats other animals for its nourishment.

producer Organisms can be categorized according to how they obtain energy to survive. *Producers* capture energy from the sun during photosynthesis. In contrast, *consumers* are animals that must consume plants or other animals to obtain their energy.

qualitative studies Experimentation in which data collection involves observations but no numerical results.

quantitative studies Experimentation in which data collection involves measurements and numerical results.

raw data Any data collected during the course of an experiment that has not been manipulated in any way.

research Also called a *literature search*. Locating and studying all existing information about a subject.

scavenger An organism that consumes dead organic matter.

scientific method The basic methodology of all scientific experimentation, including the statement of a problem to be solved or question to be answered to further science, the formulation of a hypothesis, and performing experimentation to determine if the hypothesis is true or false. The scientific method involves data collection, analysis, and conclusions.

smooth data   Raw data that has been manipulated to provide understandable information in the form of graphs or charts and represents totals, averages, and other numerical analysis.

stimulus   An event that prompts a reaction or a response.

survey collection   A collection of organisms from a certain habitat or area.

statistics   Analyzing numerical data to see if the results are significant or valid.

topsoil   The top layer of soil, which usually contains large amounts of organic matter.

variable   A factor that is changed in an experiment to test the hypothesis.

vertebrate   An animal with a backbone, including reptiles, amphibians, birds, and mammals.

Further reading

The following books can all be used for additional environmental science project ideas.

Berman, William. 1986. *Exploring with Probe and Scalpel—How to Dissect—Special Projects for Advanced Studies*. New York: Prentice Hall Press.

Bochinski, Julianne. 1991. *The Complete Handbook of Science Fair Projects*. New York: Wiley & Sons, Inc.

Byers, T.J. 1984. *20 Selected Solar Projects*. Englewood Cliffs, N.J.: Prentice-Hall, Inc.

Dashefsky, Steven H. 1995. *Zoology: 49 Science Fair Projects*. New York: TAB/McGraw-Hill.

——. 1992. *Insect Biology: 49 Science Fair Projects*. New York: TAB/McGraw-Hill.

——. 1994. *Microbiology: 49 Science Fair Projects*. New York: TAB/McGraw-Hill.

——. 1994. *Environmental Science: High-School Science Fair Experiments*. New York: TAB/McGraw-Hill.

Gutnik, Martin J. 1991. *Experiments that Explore the Greenhouse Effect*. Brookfield, Conn.: Millbrook Press.

——. 1991. *Experiments that Explore Oil Spills*. Brookfield, Conn.: Millbrook Press.

——. 1992. *Experiments that Explore Recycling*. Brookfield, Conn.: Millbrook Press.

——. 1992. *Experiments that Explore Acid Rain*. Brookfield, Conn.: Millbrook Press.

Irtz, Maxine. 1991. *Blue-Ribbon Science Fair Projects*. Blue Ridge Summit, Pa.: TAB Books.

Witherspoon, James D. 1993. *From Field to Lab: 200 Life Science Experiments for the Amateur Biologist*. Blue Ridge Summit, Pa.: TAB Books.

For an overview of environmental science terms and topics, try:

Dashefsky, H. Steven. 1993. *Environmental Literacy*. New York: Random House.

If you are new to science fairs, here are a few good books to read. They cover all aspects of entering a science fair, including everything from getting started to statistical analysis.

Bombaugh, Ruth. 1990. *Science Fair Success*. Hillside, N.J.: Enslow Publishers.
Irtz, Maxine. 1987. *Science Fair—Developing a Successful and Fun Project*. Blue Ridge Summit, Pa.: TAB Books.
Tocci, Salvatore. 1986. *How to Do a Science Fair Project*. New York: Franklin Watts.

For information about the International Science and Engineering Fairs and valuable information about adult sponsorship, write or call:

Science Service
1719 N Street, N.W.
Washington, D.C. 20036
(202) 785-2255

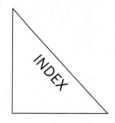

Boldface numbers indicate illustrations

About the author   H. Steven Dashefsky is an adjunct professor of environmental science at Marymount College in Tarrytown, New York. He is the founder of the Center for Environmental Literacy, which was created to educate the public and business community about environmental topics. He holds a B.S. in biology and an M.S. in entomology and is the author of more than a dozen books that simplify science and technology.